LEARNING WORKS ENRICHMENT SERIES

MONSTERS · MYSTERIES
UFOs

W9-BEV-011

WRITTEN BY LINDA SPELLMAN
ILLUSTRATED BY BEV ARMSTRONG

MAR 2009

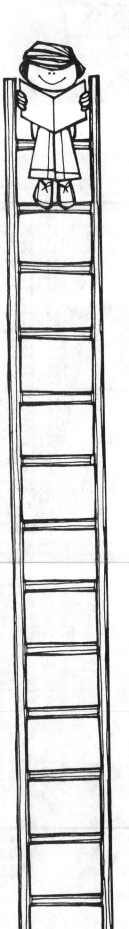

The Learning Works

Contents

Contents
(continued)

To the Teacher

The activities in this book have been selected especially for gifted students in grades 4 through 6 and are designed to help them develop and apply higher-level thinking skills. These activities have been grouped by subject matter into the following sections: monsters, mysteries, and UFOs.

Monsters

People have long been fearful of and fascinated by forces they could not equal and events they could not explain. They have imagined monsters and then have invented the means to control them. They have passed laws against vampires and werewolves, placed likenesses of griffins on shields and banners, searched the northwestern woods for Bigfoot, and waited in the chill air beside a lake for a glimpse of Nessie.

The activities in this section introduce students to famous and fabled monsters of the past and present and help them understand the roles these creatures have played in heraldry, legends, and myths.

Mysteries

The march of history has left many unanswered questions in its wake. Why did the ancient Egyptians build pyramids? What ended the Maya civilization in southern Mexico? What was the purpose of Stonehenge? Where did the stone-carving people of Easter Island come from, why did they carve great stone heads, and what stopped their work? Who or what etched geometric patterns on the ground of the Palpa Valley near Nazca in Peru? Did a now-lost continent called Atlantis ever exist and, if so, where? How did Machu Picchu, the remarkable stone city of the Incas, come to be? *Exactly* what happened to the more than one thousand people who have disappeared without a trace in the Bermuda Triangle in the past twenty-five years? Did the legendary King Arthur ever really exist?

Archaeologists and historians have searched in vain for definitive answers to these questions. The activities in this section give students opportunities to find out what the experts have learned and to formulate their own theories.

UFOs

Most unidentified flying objects (UFOs) have quickly been identified. After brief investigations, they have been found to be planets, weather balloons, earth satellites, and similar identifiable objects that were temporarily misunderstood or mistaken for something else. Some UFO sightings have been shown to be hoaxes—attempts by people to gain attention or garner publicity. But a few flying objects have remained unidentified despite extensive investigations. Were they spaceships from a civilization beneath the sea? Did they come from a distant planet or galaxy? The activities in this section enable students to examine the evidence and draw their own conclusions.

To the Teacher
(continued)

Within each of these three sections are bulletin board and learning center ideas, a pretest and a posttest, as many as fifteen activity pages, detailed directions for more than fifty activities, suggestions for additional correlated activities, an answer key, and an award to be given to students who satisfactorily complete the unit of study. These materials may be used with your entire class, for small-group instruction, or by individuals working independently at their desks or at learning centers. Although you may want to elaborate on the information presented, each activity has been described so that students can do it without additional instruction.

All of the activities in this book are designed to provide experiences and instruction that are qualitatively different and to promote development and use of higher-level thinking skills. For your convenience, these activities have been coded according to Bloom's taxonomy. The symbols used in this coding process are as follows:

●	**knowledge**	recall of specific bits of information; the student absorbs, remembers, recognizes, and responds.
■	**comprehension**	understanding of communicated material without relating it to other material; the student explains, translates, demonstrates, and interprets.
▲	**application**	using methods, concepts, principles, and theories in new situations; the student solves novel problems, demonstrates use of knowledge, and constructs.
✳	**analysis**	breaking down a communication into its constituent elements; the student discusses, uncovers, lists, and dissects.
▬	**synthesis**	putting together constituent elements or parts to form a whole; the student discusses, generalizes, relates, compares, contrasts, and abstracts.
◉	**evaluation**	judging the value of materials and methods given purposes; applying standards and criteria; the student judges and disputes.

These symbols have been placed in the left-hand margin beside the corresponding activity description. Usually, you will find only one symbol; however, some activities involve more than one level of thinking or consist of several parts, each involving a different level. In these instances, several symbols have been used.

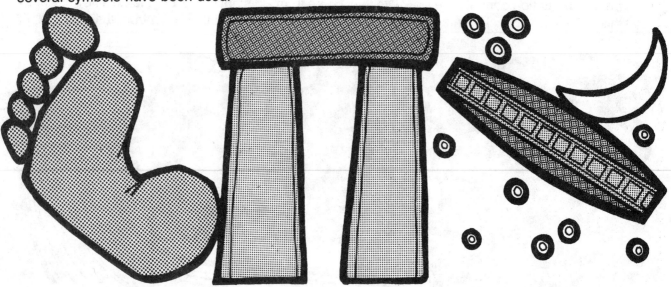

Bulletin Board Ideas

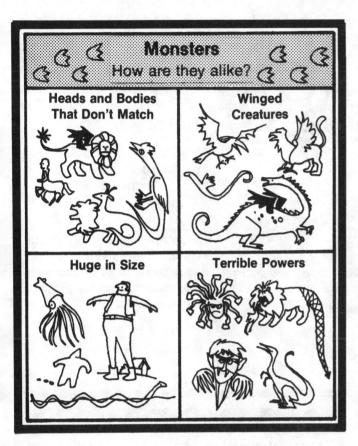

Monsters
How are they alike?

Heads and Bodies That Don't Match

Winged Creatures

Huge in Size

Terrible Powers

Monsters
"Exaggerations of Reality"

Basilisk, the Lizard

Basilisk, the Monster

Reality

Monster

Match the reality cards to the monster cards.

Famous Stories About Monsters

Write a story of your own about a monster. Illustrate it, mount it, and add it to our gallery.

St. George and the Dragon

Perseus and Medusa

Jack, the Giant Killer

King Kong

Og

Count Dracula

Learning Center Ideas

MONSTER MAGIC

1. Set up a classification system of monster attributes (physical description or characteristics, size, powers). Then classify every monster you read about according to your system.

2. Conduct a survey to see how many people believe in the existence of Bigfoot or Nessie.

3. Graph the results of your survey.

4. Make an illustrated glossary of monster descriptions.

5. Organize a Monster Day at your school. Have students dress up as monsters. Draw or take their pictures. Then put the pictures in a scrapbook.

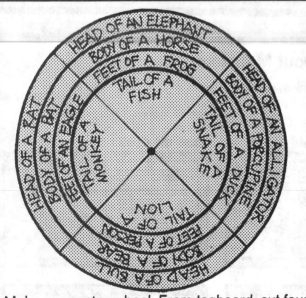

Make a monster wheel. From tagboard, cut four circles in different sizes. Divide each circle into four sections. In each section of one circle, near the outer edge, describe a different type of head. On the other circles, similarly describe types of bodies, feet, and tails. Invite class members to create monsters by spinning the wheel.

Using any kind of modeling material, sculpt figures of monsters. Add them to a classroom monster gallery.

Name _____

Pretest

Circle the letter beside the correct answer.

1. A famous Greek giant was named
   - a. Og.
   - b. Polyphemus.
   - c. Goliath.
   - d. Zeus.

2. Legend says that from the blood of Medusa's head came
   - a. writhing snakes.
   - b. Perseus.
   - c. Pegasus.
   - d. Athena.

3. The one good Centaur was
   - a. Cyclops.
   - b. Prometheus.
   - c. Hercules.
   - d. Chiron.

4. Fierce winged creatures who omitted a terrible odor were the
   - a. Harpies.
   - b. Sirens.
   - c. Cyclopes.
   - d. Striges.

5. The basilisk
   - a. had a tail with the sting of a scorpion.
   - b. had four terrible powers.
   - c. had a voice like a flute.
   - d. vomited flames from her mouth.

6. The way to protect your home from a vampire is to
   - a. hang onions and garlic over the entrance.
   - b. nail a silver crucifix over the door.
   - c. light a candle in the window.
   - d. rub charcoal over the front of the house.

7. **Lycanthropy** is the transformation of man into a
   - a. vampire.
   - b. Chimera.
   - c. werewolf.
   - d. kraken.

8. Most scientists believe that sea serpents were really giant
   - a. sea snakes.
   - b. octopuses.
   - c. sea elephants.
   - d. eels.

9. The Loch Ness monster is found in a lake in
   - a. Switzerland.
   - b. Scotland.
   - c. Ireland.
   - d. Sweden.

10. A legendary creature said to inhabit the snowy regions of the Himalayas is the
    - a. Yeti.
    - b. Bigfoot.
    - c. Sasquatch.
    - d. Grizzly.

Name _____

Monster or Myth

For thousands of years, people have believed in monsters of every size, shape, and description. Even today we have our monsters, like Bigfoot, the Abominable Snowman, and the Loch Ness monster. Are they real or are they myths?

Many monsters of long ago are now considered to be mythological, or storybook, characters. But the fact that they never really existed doesn't diminish the fascination they hold for us. As you read this, can you conjure up pictures of a dragon, a unicorn, or Medusa? For most of us, this task is easy because monsters of all kinds have been in the books we've read, the movies we've seen, and the dreams we've dreamed.

Among the earliest people to develop very specific monsters were the Greeks. Their legends and myths tell of many different kinds of monsters for their gods and heroes to vanquish. In much the same way, many monsters came into being during the Middle Ages as foes for the brave knights. You will meet many of these monsters in this unit.

Name _____

Monster or Myth Activity Sheet

● 1. Retell a favorite story about a dragon or other monster.

▲ 2. Illustrate your story when it is complete.

✳ 3. Survey twenty people to find out how many monsters they can name. Graph the results of your survey.

◉ 4. You are the editor of a local newspaper. Write an editorial to convince your readers that one of the monsters really did (or does) exist.

_____

_____

_____

_____

_____

_____

_____

_____

_____

_____

_____

_____

_____

Name _____

Giants

Giants were very tall and possessed great strength. According to legend, however, their powers ended there. The typical giant's heart was not able to pump enough blood against the pull of gravity all the way up to the giant's brain. As a result, the poor giant was left quite dumb and could be easily outwitted.

Giants were also very clumsy. Their stomachs protruded so far that they could not even see their own feet. They had extremely long arms to enable them to reach well below their enormous stomachs. Because they needed to smell odors and hear sounds that emanated near the ground, they had very long noses and very large ears. Their mouths were proportionately outsized.

Two famous giants appear in the Bible. One of them, Og, King of Bashan, had a bed nine cubits long by four cubits wide (thirteen and one-half feet by six feet). The second biblical giant, Goliath, was six cubits and a span (between nine and ten feet) in height. Goliath was so strong that he could wear two hundred pounds of bronze armor.

Greek myths tell of three monstrous giants, all sons of Poseidon, the god of the sea. These giants, the Cyclopes, were so ugly that Zeus, the ruler of the gods, sent them to work for Hephaestus, the god of fire and metal smithing, as the leading laborers on his forge.

Sailors and explorers have told of seeing giants. Magellan recorded sighting giants in Patagonia. In 1764, crew members aboard a British ship, the *Dolphin,* also saw Patagonian giants, which they described as being between seven and nine feet tall. Nearly one hundred years later, Charles Darwin, sailing on board the *Beagle,* reported seeing Patagonians. He observed that they were more than six feet tall and were the tallest race he had ever seen, but declared that they certainly were not giants.

Name _____

Giants Activity Sheet

■ 1. How long is a **cubit**? _____ How long is a **span**?_____ A seven-foot giant would be

▲ how many cubits tall? _____

■ 2. Knowing that gravity has a negative effect on giants, invent a plan to create intelligent giants.

■ 3. On a world map, find Patagonia and trace the routes of Magellan and Darwin.

● 4. Find out about the Watusi tribe in Africa. Tell why you do or do not believe that the members of
◉ this tribe are giants.

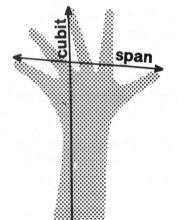

_____

_____

_____

_____

_____

_____

_____

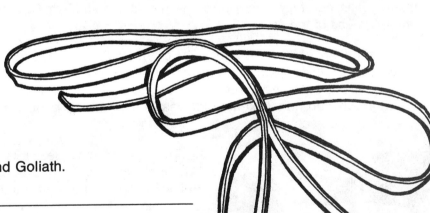

● 5. Retell the story of David and Goliath.

_____

_____

_____

_____

_____

_____

Name _____

Cyclopes

Homer was a poet who lived about three thousand years ago in Greece. He wrote **epics**, long narrative poems in which he described the adventures and deeds of historical and mythological heroes. In one of these poems, the *Odyssey,* Homer wrote about Odysseus.

Odysseus was the king of an island called Ithaca. While returning with his men by ship from a long war in Troy, he was caught in a great storm and blown off course. He found himself near the land of the Cyclopes. Odysseus and twelve of his men went ashore in this land. They found a cave filled with lambs, kids, and cheeses. The men were hungry and wanted to take all of what they had found, but Odysseus cautioned them, saying, "Wait 'til the owner of the cave returns."

At sundown, Polyphemus, a one-eyed Cyclops, returned to the cave with his sheep. After he drove the animals into the cave, he closed the entrance with a huge stone.

Uncertain what would happen, Odysseus and his men tried to hide in a corner of the cave, but Polyphemus found them. When Odysseus explained that he and his men were Greeks who had been driven there by a storm on the seas, the monster just laughed and devoured two of the men for dinner.

Odysseus thought about killing the giant, but decided little would be accomplished by doing so because he and his men would not be strong enough to move the huge stone away from the mouth of the cave. With the giant dead, they would be trapped in his cave forever.

The next morning, the giant ate two more men and then left the cave to herd his sheep in the nearby hills, carefully rolling the stone in place behind him. Odysseus and his men spent all day in the darkness of the cave.

At sundown of the second day, the giant returned and ate two more men. Then he drank some strong wine Odysseus had given him and fell into a drunken stupor. While Polyphemus slept, Odysseus and his men blinded him by sticking a red-hot poker in his eye. Then, knowing he would be furious when he awakened and realized what had happened, they again hid from him and planned their escape.

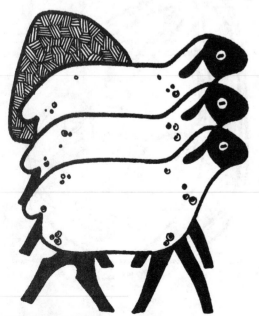

The next morning the giant awoke. At first, all he felt was pain. When he realized he had been blinded, he flew into a rage. Bellowing loudly, he vowed that none of the Greeks would get out of his cave alive.

The blinded Polyphemus groped his way to the cave entrance and rolled aside the stone to let his sheep out. As the animals passed by the giant, he carefully felt the back of each one to make sure that none of the Greeks was trying to sneak out by clinging to the sheep. But the clever Greeks were able to outsmart Polyphemus. They tied three sheep together and had one man hold onto the bottom of the middle sheep in each threesome. In this way, they were able to escape undetected from the cave and from the enraged Polyphemus and to be on their way home once again.

Name _____

Cyclopes Activity Sheet

● 1. Odysseus had other adventures and met other perils on his voyage. Find out how he tricked the Sirens and retell that story.

✱ 2. In what ways does the description of Polyphemus match and/or differ from the general description of giants given on page 12?

▲ 3. Draw a cartoon strip that tells the story of Odysseus and Polyphemus.

Name _____

Medusa

In ancient Greece, according to myth, there were three monstrous sisters, the Gorgons. Their names were Sthenno, Euryale, and Medusa. The Gorgons were terrifying creatures with the faces of women and the bodies of dragons. They had wings, claws, and tusklike teeth, and their heads were covered with writhing serpents.

Medusa, unlike her two sisters, had once been a lovely maiden much admired and envied for her beautiful hair. Because she chose to compete in beauty with the goddess Athena, Medusa was deprived of her charms. Her long, flowing tresses were transformed by the jealous goddess into hissing snakes. Everyone who looked directly at Medusa's head was changed to stone.

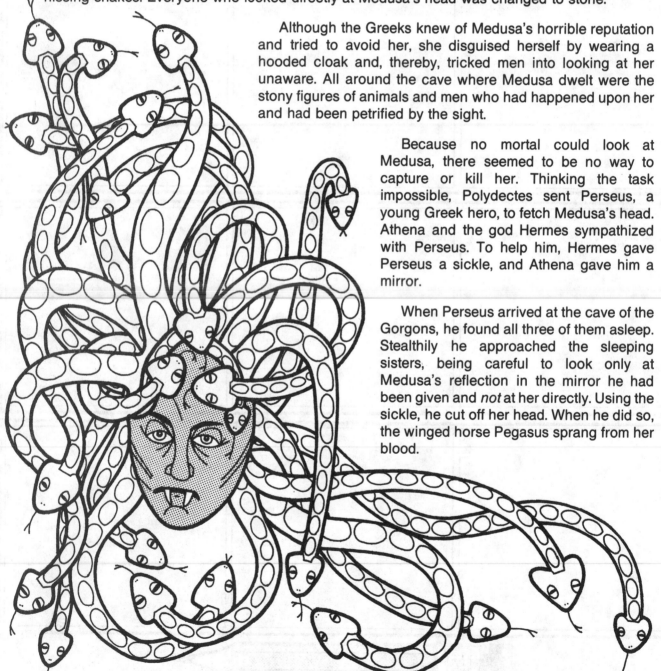

Although the Greeks knew of Medusa's horrible reputation and tried to avoid her, she disguised herself by wearing a hooded cloak and, thereby, tricked men into looking at her unaware. All around the cave where Medusa dwelt were the stony figures of animals and men who had happened upon her and had been petrified by the sight.

Because no mortal could look at Medusa, there seemed to be no way to capture or kill her. Thinking the task impossible, Polydectes sent Perseus, a young Greek hero, to fetch Medusa's head. Athena and the god Hermes sympathized with Perseus. To help him, Hermes gave Perseus a sickle, and Athena gave him a mirror.

When Perseus arrived at the cave of the Gorgons, he found all three of them asleep. Stealthily he approached the sleeping sisters, being careful to look only at Medusa's reflection in the mirror he had been given and *not* at her directly. Using the sickle, he cut off her head. When he did so, the winged horse Pegasus sprang from her blood.

Name _____

Medusa Activity Sheet

■ 1. Discover more details about Medusa and her fate.

▲ 2. Draw a picture showing Medusa sitting in her cave.

▲ 3. Using clay, sculpt a head of Medusa.

■ 4. Pretend you are a Greek storyteller. Make up a story telling how Medusa acquired some of the stony figures surrounding her cave.

Name _____

Centaurs

The Centaurs were a race of Greek monsters who were portrayed as having the torso and head of a man and the hindquarters of a horse. But the Centaurs had not always looked like that. Legend says that, originally, they were hairy, giantlike men who hunted bulls on horseback. When their weight became too great for their horses to bear, they developed their own hindquarters.

The Centaurs inhabited meadows and forests in the mountainous regions of Thessaly and Arcadia, where they built their homes among mazes of densely wooded pathways. They usually lived together in families or tribes. Fast, wild, and savage, they armed themselves with stone slabs and tree trunks and were very difficult to capture.

One Centaur, Chiron, was noted for his goodness and wisdom. He was educated by Apollo and Artemis. Apollo was the Greek god of archery, music, and medicine. Artemis was the goddess of the hunt. Their pupil Chiron was renowned for his skill in medicine, music, gymnastics, and hunting. Many distinguished Greek heroes, such as Achilles, Jason, and Heracles, became Chiron's pupils and his friends.

In a battle between the Centaurs and Heracles, one of Heracles' poisoned arrows accidently struck Chiron in the knee. Using the medical knowledge he had received from Chiron, Heracles tried to cure his former teacher but was unable to do so.

Chiron was immortal, but the pain from his wound was so great that he wanted to die. He gave his immortality to Prometheus, whereupon Zeus placed Chiron in the sky as the constellation Sagittarius.

Name _____

Centaurs Activity Sheet

■ 1. All of our stories about how monsters came to be have been handed down in legends. Create a new legend telling how the Centaurs came to be half man and half horse.

■ 2. Chiron taught many Greek heroes. Among his pupils were Achilles, Jason, Heracles, Castor, and Pollux. Find out something about each one of these men. What did he do? How did he become a hero?

Achilles _____

_____

_____

Castor _____

_____

_____

Heracles _____

_____

_____

Jason _____

_____

_____

Pollux _____

_____

_____

■ 3. The Greeks loved beautiful vases. On a separate sheet of paper, create a vase design in which you use the figure of a Centaur.

◉ 4. Discuss the qualities that make someone a good teacher. Then tell why a Centaur might or might not be a good teacher.

Name _____

The Chimera and the Harpies

Some Greek monsters brought destruction. Among them were the Chimera and the Harpies. The Chimera had heads of a lion and a goat, the body of a lion, and the tail of a dragon. She was said to inhabit the wild hills of Lycia and to spew forth terrible flames. She was finally killed by the Greek hero, Bellerophon. Riding on the back of the winged horse, Pegasus, he shot the Chimera with a bow and arrow. To this day, a volcano near Phaselis in Lycia bears her name.

The Harpies were winged creatures with the body, claws, wings, and beak of a bird, the ears of a bear, and the face of a haggard old woman. They emitted a terrible odor. They flew with the wind and used their wings as armor to protect themselves from spears and arrows.

The Harpies were robbers. They would go into homes to steal food from the table, leaving hunger, famine, and disease in their wake. Angry gods sometimes sent the Harpies to torment and punish their enemies.

Name _____

Chimera and Harpies Activity Sheet

▲ 1. According to one legend, the Chimera was born in the volcano of the same name near Phaselis in Lycia. Inside this volcano lived many strange and fearsome creatures. Near the top were lions, in the middle were goats, and at the bottom were poisonous dragons. As the Chimera was being born, it inherited characteristics from each of these creatures.

   A monster has just been born in a deep cavern beneath the sea. In the waters of this cavern live many creatures. Near the bottom are octopuses, at the middle level are sharks, and near the top and along the shore are crocodiles. This new monster has been formed in the same way as the Chimera. Imagine what this new monster might look like. In the frame below, draw a picture of it and give it a name.

● 2. Read to discover what finally happened to the Harpies. Draw a cartoon to illustrate or write a paragraph to describe what you learn.

■ 3. Make up a story about the Harpies and their evil deeds.

■ 4. In Greek mythology, the gods and goddesses had particular areas of power or responsibility. For example, Apollo was the god of archery, music, and medicine. Demeter was the goddess of the earth's fruits, especially of corn and grain. Make a table or chart on which you list the names of gods and goddesses in one column and then list their areas of power or responsibility in another column.

■ 5. In Greek mythology, Zeus is the greatest of the Olympian gods. He is the son of Cronos and Rhea and the brother of Poseidon, Hades, Demeter, and Hera. Draw a geneological chart or family tree for Zeus and some of the other Greek gods and goddesses.

Name _____

Dragons

The fearsome dragon, the legendary offspring of an eagle and a wolf, was always depicted as a huge, lizard-like creature with a head like that of an alligator. He had a long tongue and sharp teeth and could breathe poisonous fire. His body was covered with thick scales that formed an armor so hard no ordinary sword or spear could pierce it. Sometimes, dragons also had wings.

There were dragons of the air, of the land, and of the sea. All of them poisoned the waters of the world. Only the unicorn and the rhinoceros could help to eliminate the poison of the dragons from the waters.

One famous story tells how St. George slew a dragon. According to this story, a large dragon lived outside a town in Syria. Every time the dragon breathed fire over the city walls, its poison caused the death of all who were touched by it. The frightened residents of the city threw two sheep over the wall each day to appease the dragon and keep him from breathing his terrible fire.

When there were no more sheep, the people began to sacrifice one another, two at a time. They decided which of them would be sacrificed to the dragon by drawing lots. Because the victims were selected in such a fair and impartial manner, not much time elapsed before the name of a beautiful princess was drawn. Her father, the king, wanted to spare her; but the citizens insisted that she, too, must be bound by the rules of the lottery. At length, the grieving king gave in and sent his daughter to meet her death in the clutches of the dragon.

On this same day in a neighboring village, a young religious gentleman named George received a message from God telling him to go immediately to the place where the young princess awaited her terrible fate. He did so and, upon meeting the princess and hearing her woeful tale, decided to kill the dragon and save her. After slaying the beast, he returned the princess to her father and was hailed as a hero by all the people in the kingdom.

Name _____

Dragons Activity Sheet

● 1. Learn the song "Puff, the Magic Dragon" and tape yourself singing it while accompanying
■   yourself with an instrument.

▲ 2. Using clay to sculpt, build a diorama showing St. George killing the dragon and rescuing the
   princess.

■ 3. Create a legend telling how the dragon, an offspring of an eagle and a wolf, ended up looking as
   he did.

✳ 4. Compare Puff with the fearsome dragons described on page 22. How are they alike? In what
   ways are they different?

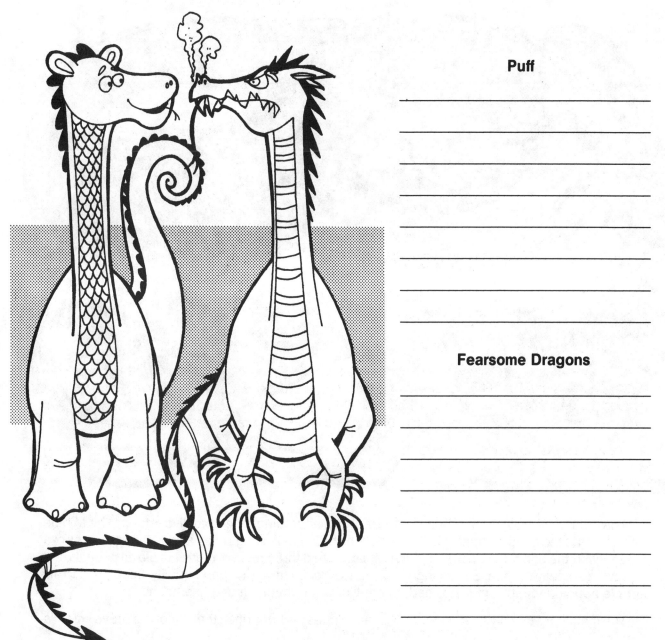

Puff

_____

_____

_____

_____

_____

_____

_____

Fearsome Dragons

_____

_____

_____

_____

_____

_____

_____

_____

Name _____

The Basilisk and the Manticore

The basilisk was a ten-foot-long, sinuous lizard that supposedly lived during the Middle Ages. King of his order, he was hatched by a serpent from the egg of a cockatrice, another legendary animal with the head, wings, and legs of a cock and the tail of a serpent. The basilisk preferred to live in hot places, preferring underground caverns near geysers or warm, tangled thickets.

The basilisk had four terrible powers. His smell was so bad that one whiff could overpower and kill. His hissing was so frightening that it scared people to death. The fire from his mouth was so hot that it burned his enemies to a crisp. And his eye was so horrible that a brief look into it would petrify the hapless viewer. The only way a brave knight could fight the basilisk was while looking at this fearsome monster's reflection in a mirror.

The manticore was another horrid monster who, according to legend, lived during the Middle Ages. He had the head of a man, the body of a lion, the leathery wings of a bat, and the spiked tail of a dragon with the sting of a scorpion. The manticore had three rows of teeth. He ate all animals, but his favorite meal was man. Surprisingly, the manticore did have one good quality. In contrast to his terrible appearance, this monster had a beautiful voice that sounded like a flute.

The manticore usually lived in wild mountain ranges and was often the object of a brave knight's search.

Name _____

Basilisk and Manticore Activity Sheet

✱ 1. The basilisk had four terrible powers. On the lines below, list the names of other monsters that had one or more of these same powers.

Odor

_____

_____

_____

Hissing

_____

_____

_____

Breath of Fire

_____

_____

_____

Petrifying Eye

_____

_____

_____

▲ 2. In the frame on the right, draw a picture of the basilisk using one of his four terrible powers to subdue an enemy.

■ 3. On a separate sheet of paper, write a paragraph in which you tell what power or quality the basilisk and Medusa had in common and compare the ways in which they were killed.

■ 4. There are no well-known stories about the manticore. Write a story in which both his bad qualities and his flutelike voice are important to the plot.

Name _____

Griffin

The griffin was a creature with head, neck, wings, and forelegs like those of an eagle, but one hundred times larger. The griffin had the body, hind legs, and tail of a lion, but eight times larger. The griffin had talons as long as the horns of an ox. Its ribs were so strong that they could be used as bows by even the strongest archers.

Griffins supposedly lived in the southern parts of Russia where they found and guarded gold and killed would-be plunderers. Ancient Indian legends say that they also guarded gold mines.

In heraldry, griffins are symbols of power and vigilance. For this reason, likenesses of them often adorned the shields and banners of knights and families in the Middle Ages and the front pillars of medieval castles.

In Lewis Carroll's whimsical story *Alice's Adventures in Wonderland,* Alice meets a griffin who dances for her. She never feels comfortable with him, however, even though he is only a mild, clumsy fellow.

Name _____

Griffin Activity Sheet

● 1. Read Lewis Carroll's *Alice's Adventures in Wonderland* to learn more about Alice's encounter with a griffin.

■ 2. The practice of creating and displaying such armorial insignia as griffins on banners and shields is known as **heraldry**. For heraldic purposes, various creatures and colors symbolized certain personal qualities. The griffin symbolized power and vigilance. The position of the creature was also important. For example, he could be **rampant**, **couchant**, or **dormant**. Do research to discover what these terms mean, what other creatures were used in heraldry, and what these creatures symbolized. When you have finished, create a picture chart to illustrate what you have learned.

■ 3. Design a medieval shield with a griffin on it.

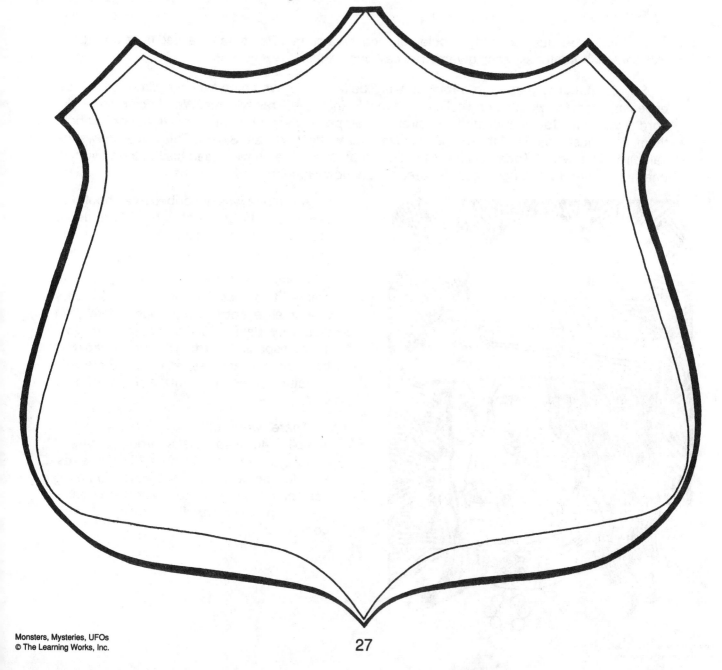

Name _____

Vampires

Vampires were beings that had once been alive, had died, and had then returned to the world of the living. In this way, they were different from ghosts, who could not reenter the world of the living.

The belief in vampires goes back to ancient Greece and the **empusas**, who took on the form of beautiful women to make men fall in love with them and marry them. Then they drank the grooms' blood as a "wedding present."

Later, people believed in the **lamias**, who lived in Africa and had three talents. They could take the form of a creature that was half woman and half snake, remove their own eyes, and drink a lot of blood.

The **striges** were a similar kind of vampire who changed into birds and drank the blood of children.

In France, because so many people believed in vampires, Parliament passed laws during the fifth and sixth centuries making vampires pay huge fines.

Several hundred years ago, vampires were believed to have come from the Slavic countries, especially from the wooded part of Romania that is known as Transylvania. Well-known poets like Lord Byron and Goethe included vampires in their poems, and other authors wrote books about them. The most famous of these books is *Dracula,* written by Bram Stoker. This novel shows the vampire at his worst. Today historians believe that Stoker may have based his book on two real characters who lived long ago in the area that is now Hungary and Romania.

A vampire was described as a ghoul who came out of his grave at night and wandered the countryside, sucking the blood of the living and transforming them into vampires.

It was said that vampires' ears had pointed tips, their hair and nails were very long, their eyebrows were bushy, their skin was very pale, and their teeth were very sharp, especially the two that protruded over their lower lip and caused the characteristic punctures they made in the necks of their victims.

There were only two ways to kill a vampire—to drive a stake through his heart or to dig him up and burn him to ashes. People who believed in and feared vampires used onion and garlic to protect their homes and wore silver crucifixes to protect their bodies.

Name _____

Vampires Activity Sheet

● 1. List all of the protections and powers that can be used against vampires.

● 2. Retell the story of Count Dracula and illustrate it.

▲ 3. Design a coffin that would be pleasing to a vampire. Remember that the vampire must be able to open it from the inside and that it must protect the vampire from exposure to the harmful rays of the sun.

▲ 4. Build the coffin in miniature of cardboard or balsa wood.

■ 5. Compare Count Dracula and an empusa. In what ways did the ideas people had about vampires change over the centuries?

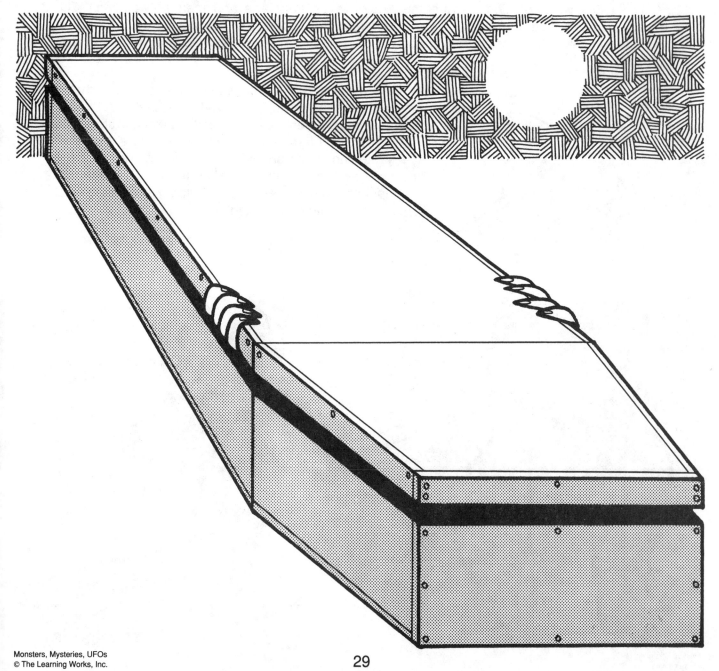

Name _____

Werewolves

Man has always been afraid of wolves, animals especially dangerous when hungry. In the Bible, the wolf was depicted as cruel and fierce. In ancient Greece, Ovid recorded an old myth about Lycaeon and how Zeus turned him into a wolf. Virgil, a Roman poet, told about a sorcerer who used poisonous herbs to turn himself into a werewolf.

In Ireland in the 1100s, a story was told of a priest and his friend who were met in their travels by a wolf. The wolf implored them to follow him, assuring them that there was nothing to fear. It appeared that the wolf had once been a man. He and his wife had been changed into wolves by another priest. The wolf wanted the priest to give the final rites to his wife, who was dying. While doing so, this priest found that there really was a woman within the she-wolf.

The word **werewolf** comes from the Anglo-Saxon language and means "wolfman." The changing of a human into a wolf is called **lycanthropy** and was once considered the work of witches with the help of the devil. Werewolves were sly, cunning, slavering beasts with voracious appetites.

One interesting characteristic of werewolves is that, if they were injured while in the wolf state, they would have the same injury when they returned to the human state. The story is told of a farmer who was attacked by a werewolf. The farmer, an extremely strong man, was able to cut off the werewolf's left paw. When he returned home, the farmer was appalled to discover his wife holding a bleeding wrist where her left hand had been.

In the sixteenth century, so many people believed in werewolves that the French Parliament passed a law forbidding the practice of lycanthropy and expelling all werewolves.

Name _____

Werewolves Activity Sheet

 1. Compare and contrast vampires and werewolves. In what ways are they similar? In what ways are they different?

_____

_____

_____

_____

_____

_____

_____

_____

_____

_____

_____

 2. What do the following words mean?

depict _____

sorcerer _____

implore _____

slavering _____

voracious _____

appalled _____

▲ 3. Make a shoe box diorama to portray the story of the priest and the wolves.

◉ 4. Pretend that you are a member of the French Parliament. Prepare and present a speech to convince other members that werewolves exist and that a law expelling them from the country is needed and must be passed. Your speech should be an impassioned plea.

Name _____

Sea Serpents

The sea serpent of the past few centuries is most interesting. In 1734, a sea serpent was described in the journal of a Norwegian priest as being thirty feet in length with a long neck, long sharp snout, flippers, and a sixty-foot-long tail. In 1745, a Norwegian bishop wrote about a voyage on a Norwegian ship during which a large sea serpent's head appeared above the surface of the water. When the monster was shot, the water around it became bloody, and the serpent disappeared.

In August of 1817, several people in Gloucester, Massachusetts, saw a huge sea serpent. They said that it was eighty to ninety feet long and had a head that was shaped like a rattlesnake's, yet was the size of a horse's. Its color was dark brown, it made slow movements, and it sank like a rock.

In 1848, sailors aboard the British ship *Daedalus* spotted an enormous serpent in the South Atlantic. The sea monster kept its head and shoulders four feet above the water's surface and was dark brown with white on the underside of its neck. When it disappeared, it sank without creating a ripple.

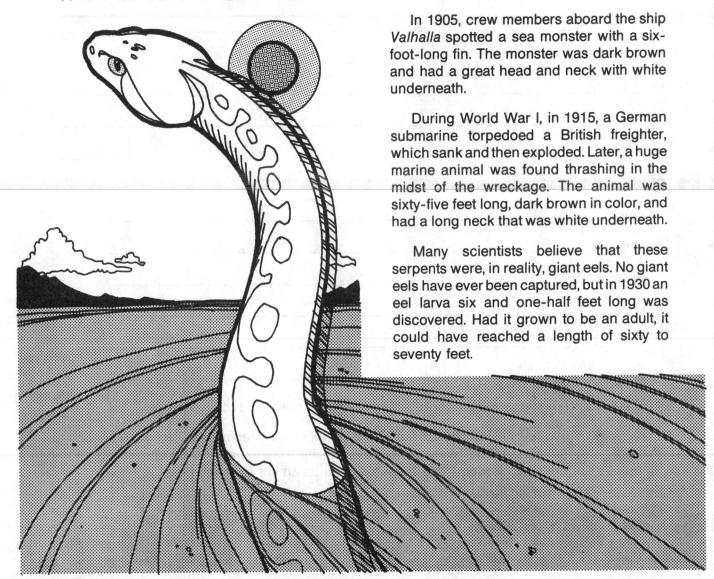

In 1905, crew members aboard the ship *Valhalla* spotted a sea monster with a six-foot-long fin. The monster was dark brown and had a great head and neck with white underneath.

During World War I, in 1915, a German submarine torpedoed a British freighter, which sank and then exploded. Later, a huge marine animal was found thrashing in the midst of the wreckage. The animal was sixty-five feet long, dark brown in color, and had a long neck that was white underneath.

Many scientists believe that these serpents were, in reality, giant eels. No giant eels have ever been captured, but in 1930 an eel larva six and one-half feet long was discovered. Had it grown to be an adult, it could have reached a length of sixty to seventy feet.

Name _____

Sea Serpents Activity Sheet

■ 1. Compare the different serpent sightings described on page 32. In what ways are they similar? In what ways are they different?

_____

_____

_____

_____

_____

_____

◉ 2. Based on these reported sightings, do you believe sea serpents really existed? State your conclusion and the facts on which it is based.

_____

_____

_____

_____

_____

_____

▲ 3. On a separate sheet of paper, draw a picture of a sea serpent as you feel it might really have looked. Label your picture to indicate the size or measurements of various body parts.

■ 4. Pretend that you are the Norwegian priest. Write a journal entry describing the sea serpent you have just seen.

_____

_____

_____

_____

_____

Name _____

Kraken

The kraken was a giant squid or octopus that made its first recorded appearance in 1555 in a book written by a Swede named Olaus Magnus, who gave a fairly accurate description of a giant squid. In 1802, Denes de Montfort gave a similar description of this huge sea monster following a long voyage.

One story is told of a boatload of fishermen who went ashore on an uncharted island. After they had begun to build a fire, the island started to sink. As the fishermen scrambled to safety, they realized to their horror that their "island" was a kraken.

A kraken was described as having a torpedo-shaped body, a slender tail, two large goggle-shaped eyes, and a parrot-like beak used for tearing apart its prey. It had ten long, slender tentacles, two of which were longer than the rest. On each tentacle were three rows of sucker-like disks.

The kraken had been seen only in Norwegian waters until November 30, 1861. On that date, sailors aboard the ship *Alecton* sighted a giant squid eighteen feet long.

In 1873, there was a kraken invasion of Newfoundland. For several months, there were numerous reported sightings along the coast.

In 1877, a "small" kraken was sent to a New York aquarium. It was more than nine feet long and had a seven-foot circumference Its eyes were eight inches in diameter, and its longest tentacles measured thirty feet.

Name _____

Kraken Activity Sheet

■ 1. Make a detailed, labeled, scientific diagram of a giant squid. Use color to enhance the diagram.

■ 2. Make a flip book depicting the fishermen landing on a kraken.

▲ 3. Sculpt a kraken using clay or bread dough.

▲ 4. Write a story set in the twentieth century about a kraken that attacks a cruise ship.

■ 5. Read to find out more about the giant squid and octopus. What do these marine animals have in common? How do their descriptions match those of the kraken?

_____

_____

_____

_____

_____

_____

_____

_____

_____

_____

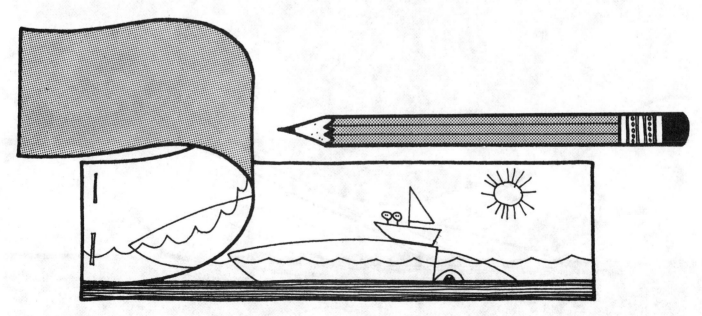

Name _____

Nessie

In Scotland, there lies a small, freshwater lake no more than twenty miles long and one and one-half miles wide. It is called Loch Ness and is connected to both the Atlantic Ocean and the North Sea by a system of canals and locks. Formed centuries ago by glaciers, this lake has steep, rocky banks and is very deep. It has an average depth of 430 feet; but at the deepest part, it is at least 754 feet deep.

Some people believe that during the Ice Age, Loch Ness was an inlet of the ocean. Later, when the water receded, a family of sea monsters might have been left behind in the lake.

Until the 1930s, there was no road close to the lake, so few people ever visited this lovely area. In 1933, a paved road was built, the lake became accessible, and a string of mysterious sightings began. In that year, as John McKay and his wife were driving along the new road, they observed a huge animal swimming in the lake. Theirs was the first of hundreds of sightings of what came to be called the Loch Ness monster.

The Loch Ness monster, sometimes affectionately nicknamed Nessie, has a small head and a long neck. Most observers report that it has a humped back, but they differ regarding the number of humps. Some claim to have seen one large hump, while others report seeing as many as nine smaller ones. Nessie's color has been described as being black, dark brown, or gray. Estimates of Nessie's length range from ten to forty feet. The monster is supposed to swim rapidly with much splashing.

Although most sightings have occurred since 1933, the first report was made in the year 565 by St. Columba, who said he had seen a man dragged bleeding and gashed from an attack by a monstrous sea serpent. When the serpent appeared again before the saint, he ordered it to disappear, which it did.

Despite numerous investigations and one underwater exploration, no solid evidence has yet been found to prove Nessie's existence.

Nessie Activity Sheet

▲ 1. Construct a diorama showing how you think Nessie and Loch Ness would look.

▲ 2. You are a reporter in the year 565. On a separate sheet of paper, write a factual account of St. Columba's encounter with a serpent for your newspaper.

■ 3. Compare Nessie with the kraken and with sea serpents. In what ways are they similar? In what ways are they different?

_____

_____

_____

_____

_____

_____

■ 4. Locate Loch Ness on a world map. Trace the connections from it to the Atlantic Ocean and to the North Sea.

◉ 5. Do you believe that sea monsters could have gotten into Loch Ness during the Ice Age? Explain why or why not.

_____

_____

_____

_____

_____

_____

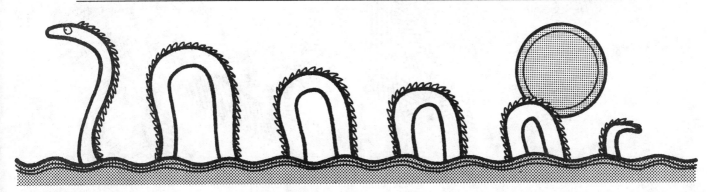

Name _____

Abominable Snowman

The Abominable Snowman, or Yeti as he is also called, is a legendary creature said to inhabit the snowy, forested regions in the Himalayas. Supposedly, he walks upright and looks to be half man and half ape. He has long, silky hair all over his body and apelike facial features.

People first became interested in the Abominable Snowman when they found large, unidentified footprints in the snow. Curiously, these footprints showed two large toes that were spread apart and three smaller toes that were close together. Since this find, many expeditions have gone to the Himalayas in search of Yeti, but they have uncovered no conclusive evidence of his existence. Scientists generally assume that the prints were made by a bear of some kind and may have been enlarged or otherwise distorted as the snow in which they lay melted.

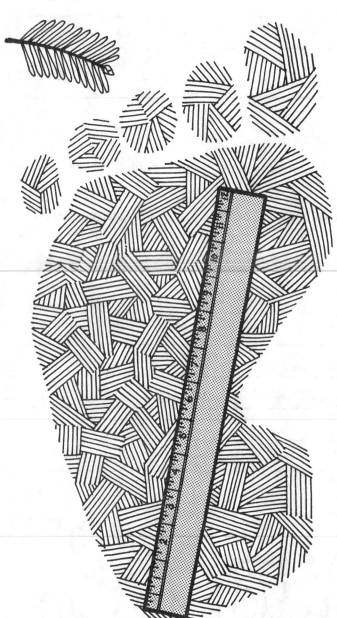

Similar to the Yeti but found in the northwestern United States and in Canada is a creature given the name of Bigfoot, or Sasquatch. This creature has been filmed by amateurs. His footprints, which have been cast in cement, range in length from fourteen to eighteen inches and in width from five and one-half to seven inches. Unlike the Yeti footprints, Bigfoot's prints show five toes of decreasing size. When Bigfoot walks, he plants his feet flat on the ground like a human.

Bigfoot has been estimated to be six and one-half to seven feet in height and is reportedly covered with dark hair except for the palms of his hands, the soles of his feet, and parts of his face. His legs are short in proportion to his torso, and his large, peaked head appears to sit directly on his shoulders.

As with the Abominable Snowman, little scientific evidence of Bigfoot has ever been found, leaving us to wonder whether or not such a creature really exists.

Name _____

Abominable Snowman Activity Sheet

✳ 1. Divide a sheet of paper into two columns. Head one column **Similarities** and the other column **Differences**. In the similarities column, list all of the ways in which Bigfoot and the Abominable Snowman are alike. In the differences column, list all of the ways in which they are different.

■ 2. Make a map of the United States and Canada. On this map, pinpoint all of the places where Bigfoot, or Sasquatch, has reportedly been sighted.

▲ 3. Make a papier mâché model of Bigfoot, incorporating as many of the reported details as possible.

■ 4. Suppose you are a news reporter. You need a good story that will sell papers, make your editor happy, and make your job with the newspaper more secure. You live in a small, northwestern town where nothing newsworthy has happened in months. You decide to make headlines with a hoax. Write a first-hand account of an imaginary Bigfoot sighting. Make your story sound convincing.

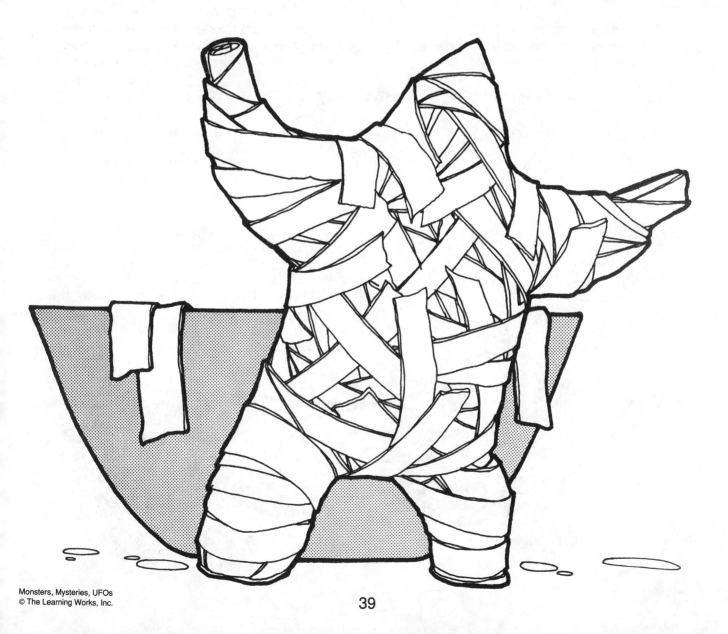

Correlated Activities

■ 1. With a small group, research some of the Greek myths about monsters. Then rewrite and illustrate these myths in a bound book for other members of your class to enjoy.

▲ 2. Make a monster mobile.

■ 3. Design a word search using the names of all of the monsters you have studied.

▲ 4. Make a poster or banner advertising a monster for sale.

▲ 5. Write and illustrate a book about the care and feeding of monsters. Include information about where they should be kept, what they should be fed, and how they can be trained or controlled.

■ 6. Write a limerick about Medusa.

■ 7. Design a maze game in which the players must find weapons or powers *before* reaching and attacking a monster.

▲ 8. Create a class Monster Museum in which to display your sculptures, dioramas, and other materials and information created and gathered during your study of monsters.

Answer Key

Pretest	Posttest
1. b	1. d
2. c	2. b
3. d	3. d
4. a	4. a
5. b	5. c
6. a	6. b
7. c	7. c
8. d	8. a
9. b	9. a
10. a	10. b

Name _____

Posttest

Circle the letter beside the answer that best completes each sentence.

1. Polyphemus was tricked by
   a. Perseus.   c. Medusa.
   b. Athena.   d. Odysseus.

2. Perseus was able to overpower Medusa by using
   a. a bow and arrow.   c. a silver crucifix.
   b. a sickle and mirror. d. garlic and onions.

3. The monster that was half man and half horse was
   a. the Chimera.   c. the Cyclops.
   b. the manticore.   d. the Centaur.

4. The Harpies used their wings as
   a. armor.   c. flame throwers.
   b. spears.   d. poisoned darts.

5. The other monster that can be killed in much the same way as Medusa is the
   a. Chimera.   c. basilisk.
   b. manticore.   d. griffin.

6. **Empusas** were vampires who drank the blood of
   a. children.   c. beautiful women.
   b. husbands.   d. other vampires.

7. The monster that suffered the same injury in both human and monster states was
   a. Dracula.   c. a werewolf.
   b. the Cyclops.   d. a griffin.

8. The monster that usually sank without a ripple was
   a. a sea serpent.   c. a kraken.
   b. the Loch Ness monster. d. a giant squid.

9. Sea monsters might have invaded Loch Ness
   a. during the Ice Age.
   b. after the road was built in 1933.
   c. during the Middle Ages.
   d. during the nineteenth century.

10. Bigfoot has reportedly been
    a. captured.
    b. filmed by amateurs.
    c. filmed by scientists.
    d. proved to be a hoax.

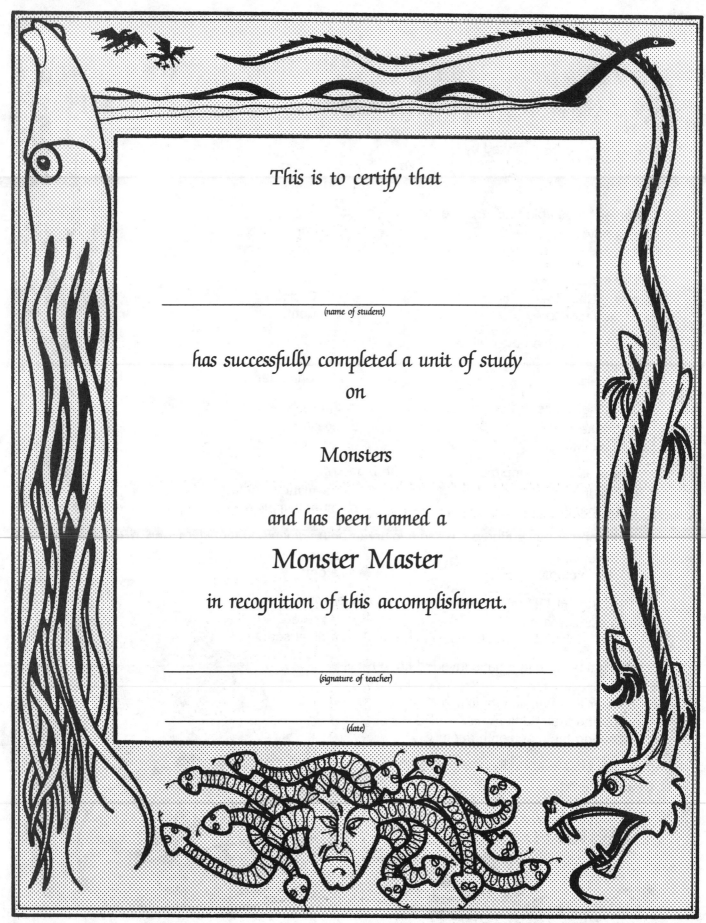

This is to certify that

_____
(name of student)

has successfully completed a unit of study
on

Monsters

and has been named a

Monster Master

in recognition of this accomplishment.

_____
(signature of teacher)

_____
(date)

Bulletin Board Ideas

A World of Mystery

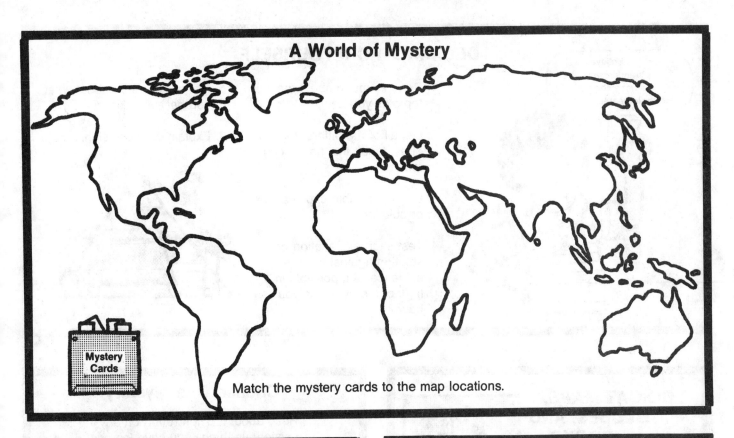

Match the mystery cards to the map locations.

Follow the Clues

and Name the Mysteries

Construction Without Metal Tools

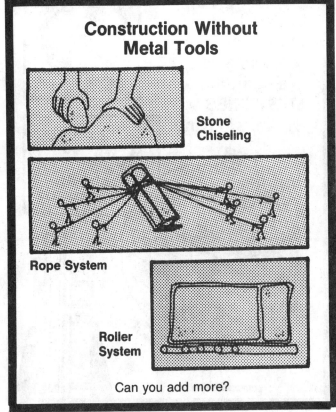

Stone Chiseling

Rope System

Roller System

Can you add more?

Learning Center Ideas

DECIDING FOR YOURSELF

I believe pyramids were the way pharaohs showed off their wealth.

1. Read as much about the topic as you can.

2. List all of the different kinds of evidence that have been found.

3. List all possible explanations or solutions.

4. Test each explanation or solution against the evidence. Is it possible in light of the evidence you have?

5. Make a decision about what you believe to be true.

6. Explain your decision.

LOOK AT MAPS, GLOBES, AND BOOKS

to see if there are relationships among the MYSTERIES we are studying.

Choose One Mystery

Read about it. Then report on any mysterious things you have learned.

Fill a can with clues to a mystery. Decorate the can. Then see how many people can figure out the mystery.

Name _____

Pretest

Circle the letter beside the answer that best completes each sentence.

1. The lost continent that sank into the sea was
   a. Machu Picchu.
   b. Stonehenge.
   c. Atlantis.

2. Easter Island is noted for its
   a. stone heads.
   b. pyramids.
   c. stone pillars.

3. The ruins left by ancient civilizations are especially amazing because we know they did not have
   a. large numbers of people.
   b. highly skilled workers.
   c. the wheel.

4. Some archaeologists feel that Crete was part of
   a. the Roman empire.
   b. Atlantis.
   c. the Devil's Triangle.

5. Knossos is the location of
   a. the Minoan temple of King Minos.
   b. the pyramid of Cheops.
   c. Mayan temples.

6. To serve as an astronomical calendar may be the purpose of
   a. Machu Picchu.
   b. Stonehenge.
   c. Easter Island.

7. Giant figures were etched into the ground at
   a. Nazca.
   b. Giza, Egypt.
   c. Crete.

8. The hieroglyphics of Easter Island resemble those
   a. in the Indus Valley of Pakistan.
   b. on the tombs of an Egyptian pyramid.
   c. on Sumerian clay tablets.

9. An **ascetic** is one who
   a. likes to be very clean.
   b. is very artistic.
   c. gives up all pleasure.

10. The Bermuda Triangle is a mystery because
    a. no one knows how it was built.
    b. many lives have been lost without explanation.
    c. it just disappeared from sight.

Name _____

Classical Atlantis

The encyclopedia describes Atlantis as a legendary myth recorded long ago by the Greek philosopher, Plato. Plato wrote about a Greek named Solon, who went to Egypt and was told of a great island continent that had disappeared into the sea 9,000 years earlier. This island continent had been a paradise with a highly advanced civilization. It had beautiful buildings with hot and cold running water and a system for sewage removal. There were baths, exercising grounds for leisure activity, and circular buildings. The homes and clothing of its residents were highly decorated. Temples were built to the gods, and various metals like gold, silver, and brass were used for ornamentation.

According to Solon, Atlantis was a fertile land, with many trees and a system of reservoirs and irrigation. Fruits and grains were especially plentiful.

The only explanation given for the disappearance of Atlantis was that a huge flood killed many, many people, and when it was over, the island paradise was gone.

Name _____

Classical Atlantis Activity Sheet

● 1. Plato wrote in Greek. Look under **alphabet** in a dictionary or encyclopedia to find the Greek alphabet. Write each letter and its name on a line in the chart below.

Greek Alphabet

Letter	Name	Letter	Name
A a	alpha		
B β	beta		

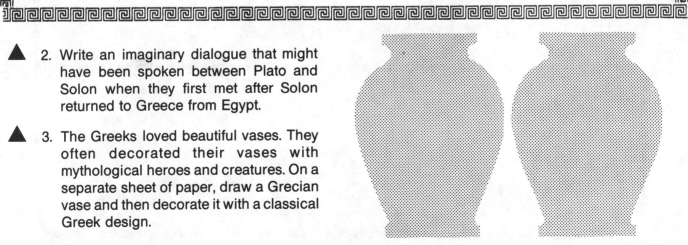

▲ 2. Write an imaginary dialogue that might have been spoken between Plato and Solon when they first met after Solon returned to Greece from Egypt.

▲ 3. The Greeks loved beautiful vases. They often decorated their vases with mythological heroes and creatures. On a separate sheet of paper, draw a Grecian vase and then decorate it with a classical Greek design.

Name _____

Atlantis of the Atlantic

Solon, in his description of Atlantis, gave very detailed dimensions for the sunken continent. When Plato recorded the story, he repeated these dimensions, which he said made the continent larger than Africa (which he called Libya) and Asia put together—so large, in fact, that it could not have been in the Mediterranean Sea but had to have been beyond the Pillars of Hercules (two opposite promontories at the entrance to the Mediterranean Sea, which today are called Gibraltar and Mount Hacho). Plato also commented that Atlantis acted as a "stepping stone" to the "opposite" continent.

For these and other reasons, many archaeologists once believed that the so-called lost continent of Atlantis was located in the Atlantic Ocean between the continents of Europe and Africa and the Americas. Many of the peoples who live along the shores of the Atlantic have legends about a big flood and the sinking of an island paradise. In times past, they even called this sunken paradise by similar names. For example, the Welsh called it *Avalon,* the Aztecs called it *Aztlan,* the Egyptians called it *Aalu,* and the Babylonians called it *Aralu.* Tribes in the Canary Islands (said by some to be the tops of Atlantis) called it *Atlantioi.* In ancient times, Canary Island cave dwellers told the Romans about the continent's sinking.

Searches have been undertaken, but the elusive Atlantis has yet to be found in the Atlantic Ocean or elsewhere.

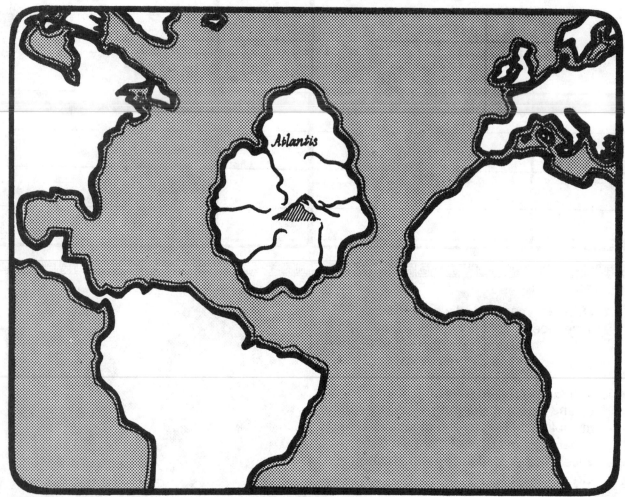

Name _____

Atlantis of the Atlantic Activity Sheet

▲ 1. Draw a map of the Atlantic Ocean. Include the Americas, Europe, and Africa. Indicate where the lost continent of Atlantis might have been. Label Greece, Egypt, Gibraltar, Mount Hacho, and the Mediterranean Sea.

■ 2. Pretend that you are a native of one of the countries along the shores of the Atlantic Ocean. Write down the legend of the big flood and the disappearing land as it might have been told to you.

◉ 3. Using an atlas, study the depths of the Atlantic Ocean. Does there seem to be a large area of the ocean floor that is higher than the rest and might be a sunken land mass? Explain your answer.

▲ 4. In the frame below, draw a landscape. Include at least five things you would find in a paradise.

Name _____

Mediterranean Atlantis

Today some archaeologists say that, because of a simple mathematical error, the search for Atlantis has been in the wrong place. They claim that Atlantis was in the Mediterranean Sea and was a Minoan civilization. In 1500 B.C., a great catastrophe, probably an earthquake or a volcanic eruption, hit that area, causing much of it to sink. Today, Crete is all that remains of this ancient civilization.

When scholars reviewed Solan's description, they found that it fit much of what we know about the Minoan civilization from the ruins at Knossos. The Minoans did have hot and cold running water and a sewer system. They did use metals and paints for decoration, they built temples to their gods, and they had reservoirs and irrigation systems. In addition, a position in the Mediterranean would make Atlantis a "stepping stone" between Africa and Europe, the "opposite" continent.

The major problem of matching Solon's description to an island located in the Mediterranean is one of numbers. Solon went to Egypt in 600 B.C. and said that the sinking had occurred 9,000 years earlier, but the Minoan catastrophe had taken place only 900 years before. The dimensions of the Royal City of Atlantis match those of a city on Crete except that they are ten times too big. In fact, the problem may be an inexplicable confusion between *hundreds* and *thousands*. If Solon had misunderstood or mistranslated Egyptian numbers and, as a result, had recorded *thousands* instead of *hundreds,* then the date and dimensions would fit an Atlantis in the Mediterranean.

Who's mistaken? Was it Solon or is it today's archaeologists?

Name _____

Mediterranean Atlantis Activity Sheet

▲ 1. Draw a picture of the volcanic eruption that may have destroyed Mediterranean Atlantis in 1500 B.C.

▲ 2. Find a picture of the ruins at Knossos. Based on that picture, construct a model showing what the palace of King Minos might have looked like.

■ 3. Design a primitive system that might have been built between 3000 and 1500 B.C. to bring running water to a city. Remember that pipe had not yet been invented.

◉ 4. Might Solon have made an error in translation that caused all *hundreds* to be read as *thousands*? If so, might Atlantis have been in the Mediterranean Sea instead of the Atlantic Ocean? Explain and justify your answers.

Name _____

The Mystery of the Minoans

In the Mediterranean Sea south of Greece lies the island of Crete. Long ago, this island was inhabited by a group of Greeks whom we called Minoans. They were ruled by King Minos, and theirs was the first civilization in Europe—a civilization that reached its zenith between 3000 and 1500 B.C.

No one knows where the Minoans originally came from, when they arrived, what language they spoke, or what their written words mean. Excavations of their ruined city of Knossos show us their magnificent palaces and luxurious villas, their multistoried homes with running water, and an elaborate drainage and sewer system.

Apparently, the Minoans had a huge fleet of ships. They traded around the world, bringing back gold, ivory, and gems. With these treasures, their artisans made beautiful jewelry. They also created fine pottery and decorated the walls of their homes and temples with exciting frescoes.

Then something happened, and the people mysteriously abandoned their beautiful city. We don't know why. They may have been attacked by another group of Greeks, or an earthquake or volcanic eruption may have caused them to flee. Their magnificent city became covered with centuries of dirt, but their civilization was not forgotten. It was faithfully described in the stories that were told and retold.

In 800 B.C., the Greek poet Homer wrote about the great city of Knossos, which had been ruled by King Minos. Most people who read his story thought that it was fiction, but in 1900 a curious archaeologist named Arthur Evans bought the mound that was supposed to be the site of the legendary city of Knossos and began to dig. Over the next twenty-five years, he unearthed and restored much of that fantastic city and discovered that its existence was fact.

Name _____

Minoans Activity Sheet

● 1. Homer's story of King Minos is well known. Find it in an encyclopedia. Retell the story in the cartoon strip frames below.

◉ 2. Pretend that you are a Greek in Homer's time. Having read Homer's story of King Minos, tell whether you consider the story to be fact or fiction. Give reasons for your decision.

■ 3. Locate Crete on a map of the Mediterranean. If it had been part of Atlantis, demonstrate how Atlantis would have been a stepping stone between Africa and Europe.

■ 4. Pretend that you are Arthur Evans. On the diary pages below, record some of your feelings about your discovery of Knossos. Remember that many people disagreed with your theory and thought you were foolish to spend your money on a mound and your time in search of a fictional city.

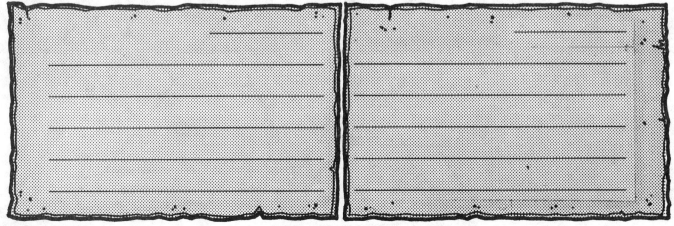

Name _____

A Peek at Pyramids

Pyramids have filled people with wonder for more than five thousand years. Many of the curious are now gone, but the pyramids still stand after centuries of wind, decay, tourists, wars, tomb robbers, and earthquakes.

Millions of people have read about, visited, and studied the pyramids in detail; but their construction and purpose remain a mystery. We do know that the Egyptian pyramids consisted of a square base and four triangular sides that met in a point at the top. Their construction was based on mathematical theories that had not yet been invented and employed engineering skills so precise that the Egyptians were able to level the walls perfectly and to line up their pyramids directly with the North Star.

These amazing pyramids were built of millions of stone blocks, each weighing fifteen tons or more. No one knows how these stones were quarried, moved, or shaped because the Egyptians had no iron tools, no horses, and no wheels.

Many pyramids are of immense size, not in proportion to human size as has been most architecture throughout history. The largest pyramid of all, built by Cheops, spreads across thirteen acres of desert. The size of the pyramids might indicate the very high regard in which the Egyptians held their gods.

Many reasons have been given for the existence of the pyramids. The Roman historian Pliny felt that they were just a fancy and foolish way for an Egyptian ruler, or pharaoh, to show off his immense wealth. Other ancient writers suggested that they were huge storage buildings for grain. The Arabs believed that they were storehouses of wisdom and riches. More recently, scholars have thought that they were built as tombs for powerful rulers, but this belief is disappearing because archaeologists have found two and three pyramids built for one pharaoh and have found some pyramids that do not contain bodies of any pharaohs. Some people have suggested that occult forces exist in pyramids, giving them the power to grow plants better and preserve food and bodies. Theorists have even proposed that the pyramids are lookout towers and landing pads left by ancient astronauts.

As you can see, the theories are endless, and indisputable proof for any one of them is lacking. Do you have a theory of your own?

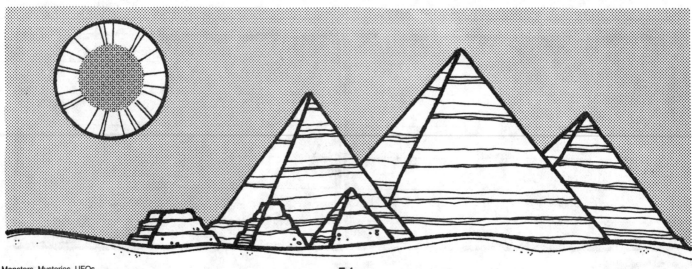

Name _____

Pyramids Activity Sheet

■ 1. Draw and label a cutaway view of a pyramid.

▲ 2. Using sugar cubes or clay blocks, construct a model of a pyramid.

▲ 3. Construct a model of the pyramids and sphinx at Giza.

■ 4. Draw a series of diagrams to show how the huge stones used to build the pyramids might have been quarried, moved, shaped, and lifted into place. Remember that the Egyptians did not have iron tools, horses, and wheels. They did, however, have slave labor.

■ 5. The true pyramid exists only in Egypt, but the term pyramid has been applied to similar structures built in other countries. Such pyramidal structures were built by the Assyrians in western Asia and by the Maya of Central America and Mexico. The Romans built small pyramid tombs. Compare the style of the pyramids built in Mexico with the style of those built in Egypt. How are they similar? How are they different?

■ 6. Write a description of what you might see if you entered an Egyptian tomb.

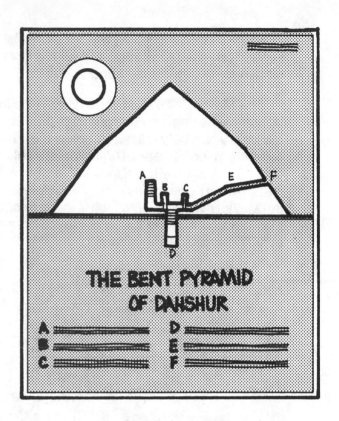

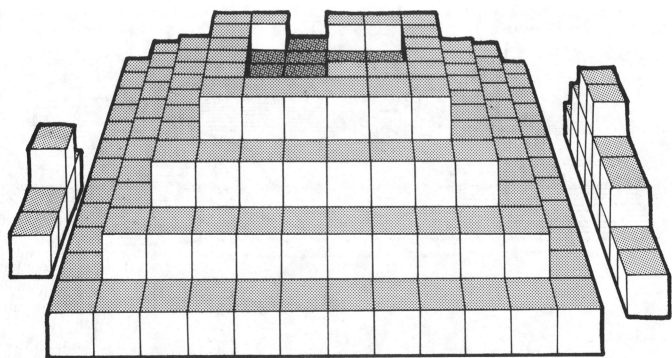

Name _____

The Missing Maya

In the sixteenth century, when the Spanish arrived in the southern part of Mexico, the Maya had already vanished. Only ruins of their highly developed civilization remained. Most of these ruins lay hidden for another three hundred years.

The Mayan civilization began to develop in 2500 B.C. Basically agricultural, it was characterized by some amazing accomplishments. For example, the Maya used a zero in their mathematics six hundred years before the Europeans did. They developed a calendar that was more accurate than our own. In fact, it was not until we were able to use computers that we realized how accurate their calendar was. They had a form of hieroglyphic writing, which is found both on stone and on a paper made from tree bark. They built beautiful step-pyramid temples. Unlike their Egyptian counterparts, the Mayan pyramids were built in steep, receding blocks and topped by ritual chambers. The Maya also devised a game that was played on a court with a ball made of rubber strips. The players actually wore special uniforms.

The Maya had a highly organized political system with leaders, armies, and workers. Yet between A.D. 800 and 900, everything just stopped, and the Maya moved out. What brought an end to their civilization? Was it disease? War? Famine? No one knows for sure.

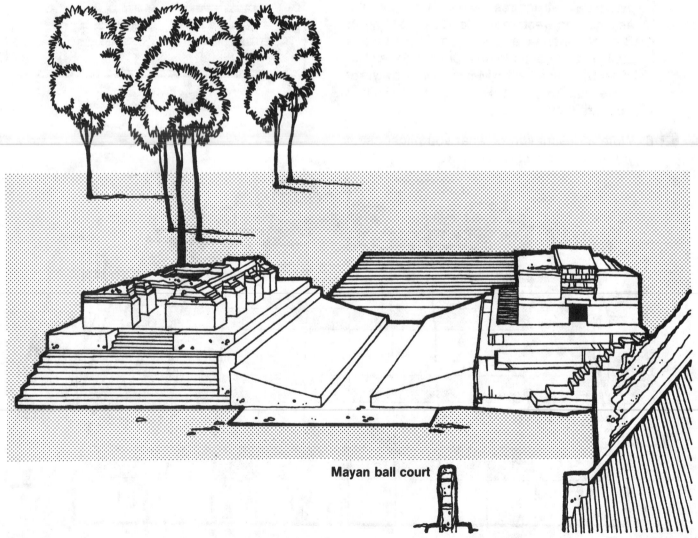

Mayan ball court

Name _____

Maya Activity Sheet

▲ 1. If you were a Mayan child, what rules would you make up for a ball game to be played on the court illustrated on page 56?

Ball Game Rules

_____

_____

_____

_____

_____

_____

_____

▲ 2. Find a picture of the Mayan calendar and study it. Then create a clay calendar. Use your own hieroglyphics to indicate the months, days, and numbers.

■ 3. Draw a picture of the step pyramid at Palenque.

■ 4. Make up a hieroglyphic code. Use it to write a letter to your friend. Draw or write your code on the lines below.

A	B	C	D	E	F	G	H	I	J	K	L
M	N	O	P	Q	R	S	T	U	V	W	X
Y	Z										

Name _____

Circle of Stones

On a lonely plain northwest of Salisbury, England, stands a circle of stone pillars. Stonemasons don't know how they were cut, engineers don't know how they were erected, and anthropologists and archaeologists don't know why they were put there.

This mysterious circle of stones is called Stonehenge, which means "hanging rocks." Using a process known as carbon-14 dating, scientists have estimated that Stonehenge was built 3,700 years ago. It consists of an outer circle of thirty massive, gray sandstone blocks, an inner circle of smaller blue stones, two concentric groups of stones laid in a horseshoe pattern, and a fifteen-foot flat block of sandstone placed in the center. This central block of stone may have been used as an altar.

The thirty pillars in the outer circle are each approximately thirty feet tall and weigh almost forty tons. These pillars serve as columns, or posts. On them rest smaller stone blocks called lintels.

Because there are no sandstone quarries near Stonehenge, the large pillar stones must have been transported no fewer than 24 miles. The builders of Stonehenge did not have horses, carts, or wheels. They probably used sledges to move these large stones. Engineers estimate that eight hundred men would have been needed to move one pillar stone in this manner.

The blue stones in the inner circle each weigh five tons. These smaller stones probably were brought by land and sea from Wales, a distance of 250 miles.

All of the stones have been carefully shaped. Because the people who cut and shaped these rocks did not have metal tools, they must have used smaller stones to chip away at the large ones. Painstakingly, they fashioned the pillars with knobs on top. Then they notched each lintel piece to match so that the stones could be locked in place.

Lifting the carved stones into place must have been an incredibly difficult task. A system of ropes was probably used to pull each of the pillar stones erect. Then heavy scaffolding of some sort might have been erected so that the lintel could be raised above the pillars, or posts, and set in place. Without tools or pulleys, the work would have been long and tedious.

Why was this monument built? Some authorities point to the altar and say Stonehenge was erected for religious reasons and may have been the site of services in which the devil or pagan gods were worshiped. Other authorities believe it was a burial ground. Still others believe that it was a giant calendar used to predict the seasons, eclipses, and other astronomical occurrences. Scientists have found that the stones are positioned such that the shadows they cast make very precise patterns, but no one knows the purpose of this system of megaliths.

Name _____

Circle of Stones Activity Sheet

■ 1. Make a diagram showing the placement of stones at Stonehenge. Then write a description of what you think their purpose might have been.

■ 2. Using a map of Great Britain, figure the distances by land and sea to transport the blue stones from Wales to the plain near Salisbury, England. Determine the best route and develop two plans for moving the stones, one using the tools and means of transportation available today and the other using what would have been available 3,700 years ago.

▲ 3. Using clay or soap, sculpt two posts with knobs on the top and a notched lintel to place on top of them.

▲ 4. When your sculpted posts are dry, tie two threads on each one. Then, holding one thread in each hand, slowly raise each post to a vertical position. As you do so, imagine how difficult it would have been to use ropes to raise a stone that weighed forty tons.

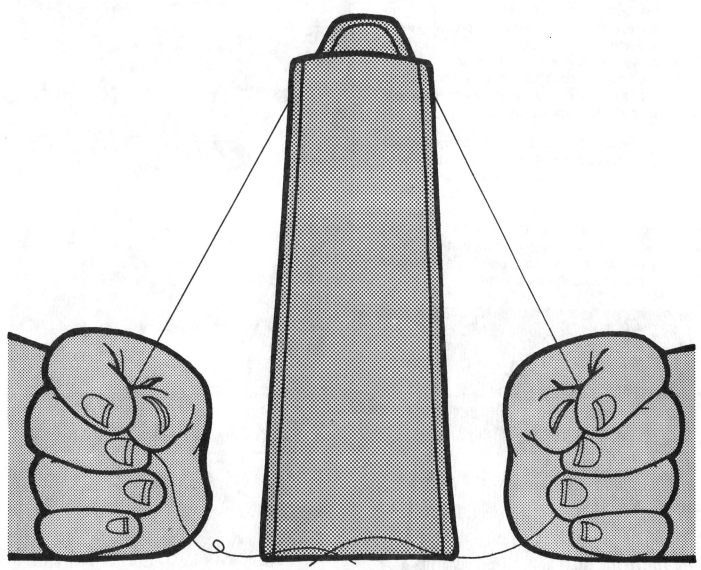

Name _____

Easter Island I

In 1721, sailors for the Dutch West India Company landed on Easter Island. They reported finding very primitive people who lived in crude huts and sailed in rough, uncalked canoes. They said that the only significant items to be seen on the island were large stone statues. Later, in 1774, Captain James Cook, an English mariner and explorer, recounted similar findings. He also reported seeing the foundations of a lost city and evidence of altars used for the worship of idols.

More than two hundred years after their discovery, the giant stone statues on Easter Island can be described but not explained. They are of several kinds. One is a megalith with a main body and a separate topknot of red stone resembling a basket. This statue is called a *moai* and sits on a platform called an *ahu.* A second type of figure is similar to the first but with a sharp, elongated face and no topknot. The third type of figure is a monolith made of basalt. It is a one-piece crouching figure with more rounded features.

Apparently, the islanders had few tools. They used obsidian to carve and shape the massive stones. Because they had no pulleys, carts, or wheels, they probably used a system of sledges atop smooth logs to move the stones from the quarry to where they now stand. Then, they may have used ropes to lift the rocks, which weighed twenty to thirty tons apiece, into place.

Most of the stone from which the statues were carved came from a quarry in the crater of the volcano Rano Raraku. High on the side of this crater, archaeologists have found workshops with statues in all stages of construction. The statues have been left unfinished, as if the workers just put down their tools at the end of one day's work and never picked them up again.

Name _____

Easter Island I Activity Sheet

▲ 1. From 1772 to 1775, Captain James Cook conducted an expedition in search of the great southern continent then believed to exist. It was during this voyage that he visited Easter Island. Read about the other places he visited. Then draw a map of the world. On it trace Cook's route and mark his discoveries.

■ 2. Make a mini-dictionary. In it write definitions for the terms listed below. Illustrate some of your definitions.

archaeologist	hieroglyphics	monolith
civilization	idols	pagan
elongated	megalith	primitive

▲ 3. Carefully sculpt a bar of soap into a head shaped like one of those found on Easter Island. As you work, you will probably be using a knife with a metal blade to shape material that is relatively soft. Remember that the people who carved the great stone statues on Easter Island shaped material that was very hard *without* metal tools.

▲ 4. Create a miniature sledge roller. Then demonstrate how such a device can be used to move a heavy load.

■ 5. Pretend that you are Captain James Cook and have recently visited Easter Island. Write a letter in which you describe what you saw to your family and friends back home.

Name _____

Easter Island II

Where did the statue-carving people of Easter Island come from? For many years, scientists thought that they had sailed *east* from Malaysia, as had the peoples of many other South Pacific islands. Recently, however, there has been a growing belief that the Easter Islanders sailed *west* from Peru.

As evidence to support this theory, scientists cite four facts. First, a Norwegian explorer named Thor Heyerdahl, believing that the inhabitants of Easter Island had sailed west from Peru in reed boats long before the time of the Incas, built a reed boat, which he named *Kon-Tiki,* and sailed west in it from Peru. He was able not only to reach Easter Island but also to sail many miles beyond, thus proving that such a voyage was possible. Second, the Indians of Peru who live near Lake Titicaca build canoes of a particular reed called totora. The only place this reed grows outside Peru in the Pacific Ocean area is in the crater of a volcano on Easter Island. Third, the stonework on Easter Island is comparable in quality to the work of the Incas at Tiahuanaco near Lake Titicaca. Fourth, there is a great similarity between the language of the Easter Islanders and that of the Incas, especially in the words used to name everyday objects.

While the inhabitants of Easter Island may have come from Peru, yet another mystery exists. Engraved on some of the statues and on the Rongo-Rongo wood tablets unearthed on the island are hieroglyphics that closely resemble those found in the Indus Valley of Pakistan, which just happens to be in the exact opposite position on the globe from Easter Island. In light of the great distance between these two points, how can this similarity be explained?

Name _____

Easter Island II Activity Sheet

▲ 1. Construct a miniature reed boat or raft. See if you can sail it on water.

● 2. Using a globe, locate the Indus Valley in Pakistan and Easter Island in the South Pacific. Is one directly opposite the other?

▲ 3. Draw a picture showing either an Easter Island landscape or the workshop inside the Rano Raraku crater.

■ 4. On a map, trace the route the islanders probably would have taken had they sailed west from Peru.

● 5. Read the book entitled *Kon-Tiki,* in which Thor Heyerdahl describes his voyage in a reed boat.

■ 6. Write a story telling what it would be like to cross the vast Pacific Ocean in a tiny reed boat.

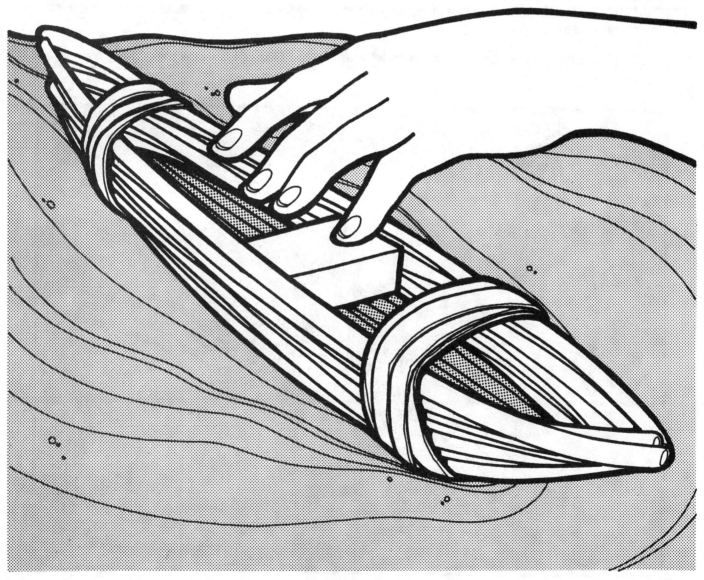

Name _____

Lines of Nazca

For many years, people knew there were deep lines etched on the ground in the Palpa Valley near the ancient city of Nazca, 250 miles southeast of Lima, Peru; but because the lines did not seem to follow any special pattern or to have any discernible purpose, they were ignored. With the advent of the airplane, however, an amazing discovery was made. From the air, it could be seen that the lines formed giant patterns, designs, or symbols.

The lines cover an area that is about forty miles long and one mile wide. They appear to be geometrically arranged. Some of them are parallel while others intersect, forming trilaterals and quadrilaterals. The lines that are straight remain straight, as if surveyed, even when they go over ridges and hills.

Some people believe that there is a direct relationship between the lines on the plain near Nazca and astronomy. They theorize that these lines, drawn about A.D. 500, are a huge astronomical chart. They view this chart as some sort of message from the Indians to their gods. Other people note that some ancient artifacts found in the same region carry pictures of objects resembling jet airplanes and feel that the Nazca lines point to landing strips high in the Andes Mountains, which were used by ancient astronauts.

Because there is no written record to tell us why the Nazca lines are there, they remain a mystery.

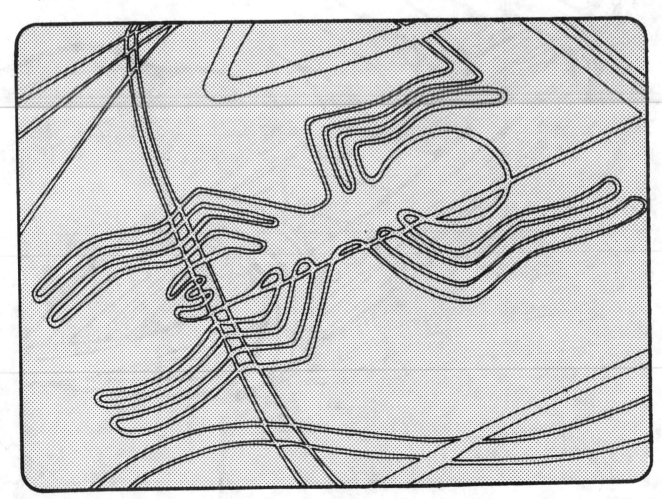

Lines of Nazca Activity Sheet

▲ 1. Pretend that you want to etch a spider on a valley or desert floor. You want the spider to be huge—500 feet long and 200 feet wide—so that it can be seen by gods in the heavens. You have no airplane or helicopter, so you cannot go up in the sky periodically to check your work. Write a detailed plan explaining how you would execute this project.

■ 2. Find pictures of some of the figures at Nazca. Choose one figure and create a legend about it in the same way the Peruvian Indians might have done.

▲ 3. Design simple line patterns to represent these three animals.

bird	**fish**	**lion**

▲ 4. If the lines on the Palpa Valley floor were an astronomical chart, what constellations in the sky could be represented by line drawings on the earth?

Constellation	**Line Drawing**
Draco	*dragon*

Name _____

Machu Picchu

In 1911, archaeologist Hiram Bingham was searching for ancient Inca cities. He was traveling along a recently blasted road near the Urubamba River in Peru when he came upon some Inca Indians who lived nearby. From them he learned that there were Inca ruins high on a mountain where fields were being cultivated. For fifty cents the Indians agreed to guide him up the mountain to a flat cliff top two hundred feet above the river—a cliff top surrounded on three sides by steep mountains.

There Bingham came upon a magnificent ruined city deserted many centuries earlier by the Incas. The buildings were constructed with huge stones, which had to have been brought many miles from the nearest quarry—across mountains, over raging rivers, and up steep inclines to the top of the cliff. Usually of granite, these rocks weighed twenty to fifty tons each. Yet the Incas had no horses, carts, or even the wheel to help them do the work.

Before the stones were put into place, the Incas carefully cut them so that they would interlock perfectly in a jigsaw pattern. Some stones had as many as thirty-two different matching surfaces and were so closely fitted that today even the thinnest knife blade cannot be placed between them. Yet, according to the artifacts that have been found, the Incas had no tools other than stones to use for chipping.

This remarkable city is called Machu Picchu. How did it come to be? Legend says that the stone "flew" to the site. Some people say ancient astronauts helped with construction. Ancient legend also says that the Incas had discovered a plant that could be used to soften rock so that it could be pushed together like putty before it hardened again.

What do you believe?

Name _____

Machu Picchu Activity Sheet

▲ 1. First mold clay into large stones. Then, cut and reshape the stones so that they will interlock. Finally, build a wall by interlocking the stones.

◉ 2. The Inca legends say that the Indians found a plant that could be used to soften rock. Tell why you do or do not believe this legend.

● 3. Archaeologists tell us that the stones were interlocked so earthquakes would not dislodge them.
■ Do research to find out if Peru has a history of earthquakes. Record and report your findings.

■ 4. Pretend that you are a newspaper reporter assigned to cover Machu Picchu. Write a factual account (telling who, what, when, where, why, how) of Hiram Bingham's discovery.

✱ 5. You have studied several ancient civilizations about which mysteries exist. Classify them on the chart below.

No Horse or Wheel

_____

_____

_____

_____

_____

No Stone Tool

_____

_____

_____

_____

_____

Moved Huge Rocks

_____

_____

_____

_____

People Disappeared

_____

_____

_____

_____

Name _____

Lost at Sea

In an area east of Florida and north of Cuba and Puerto Rico, lies a large section of ocean sometimes called the Bermuda Triangle or the Devil's Triangle. For many years, planes and ships have vanished in this area—more than one hundred since 1945—and more than one thousand lives have been lost without a single body or piece of wreckage ever being found.

These disappearances are especially mysterious because the ships and planes have vanished while in radio contact, during ideal weather, and without apparent mechanical problems. Crewmen aboard have radioed cryptic messages or have observed that the ocean "looks funny," but none have lived to tell what they saw or to explain what happened.

Strange reasons have been given for these mysterious disappearances. One theory says that an underground volcanic explosion or earthquake occurred and that the ensuing tidal wave simply overwhelmed or swallowed up any ships in the area. Another theory suggests that giant fireballs exploded the planes. Science-fiction enthusiasts say that the ships and planes were caught in a giant time-space warp, mention a possible populated underground continent, or view the disappearances as the work of huge sea monsters or of aliens from outer space.

Another unusual occurrence in this part of the world is the "white water" first reported by Columbus and later mentioned by the *Apollo 12* astronauts, who claimed it was the last light they saw from earth as they went into space. This white water is actually giant streaks of light below the surface of the ocean. In the past, it was believed that these light streaks were created by large schools of luminescent fish, but people who believe in UFOs say the streaks are searchlights from an undersea station for aliens.

Most well known of all the Triangle disappearances is that of Flight 19, five navy planes on a routine mission in 1945. Their flight plan was triangular in shape, east to the sea from Florida, then north, and finally west back to the base; but the planes never completed their mission. These five torpedo bombers, carrying plenty of fuel, flying in ideal weather, and maintaining constant radio contact, disappeared without a trace, as did the navy search plane sent out to find them. During final radio contact, the flight leader reported that he was lost, everything was wrong, he couldn't see land, he couldn't tell which direction was west, his compasses were all going crazy, and even the ocean didn't look right! Nothing more was ever heard from Flight 19.

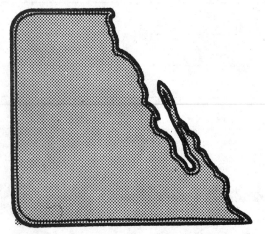
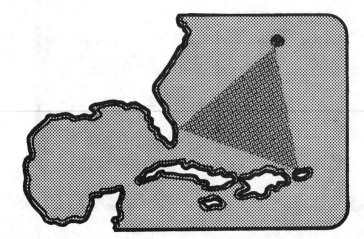

Name _____

Lost at Sea Activity Sheet

■ 1. Write a dramatization of the last communication from Flight 19.

● 2. Find out about the major ships and planes that have been lost in the Bermuda Triangle. Make a
✱ chart on which you list these losses in chronological order and briefly describe the circumstances accompanying each loss.

■ 3. Most of the disappearances have taken place between December and March. Give a reason for
this.

▲ 4. Make a salt-and-flour map of the Atlantic Ocean area showing the Bermuda Triangle. Place
markers on the map to depict planes and ships that have been lost.

◉ 5. Compare the explanations given for disappearances in the Bermuda Triangle. Tell which one
you think is the most reasonable and why you think so.

■ 6. Do research to find out about luminescence in fish or phosphorescence in water. Record and
report your findings.

Name _____

People Without Pain

Men have often marveled at the ability of those who lie on nails or walk on fire without seeming to feel pain. Who are these people and how is it done?

One group of people who can perform these amazing feats are the fakirs. *Fakir* means "poor man" in Arabic and is a name given to members of two religious groups, Muslim and Hindu, who live in the Arab lands and in India. Many fakirs live under strict rules at monasteries, devoting their lives to prayer and meditation. One group of fakirs, however, is not genuinely religious. Members of this group perform magic tricks, juggle, and practice hypnosis and ventriloquism. It is through a type of hypnosis that they are able to lie upon beds of nails and to walk barefoot on hot coals. Because of their magic, however, they are often confused with "fakers," or tricksters.

Other groups of fakirs practice **asceticism**, which means giving up personal pleasures and enjoyment to reach a higher level of life. Among the ascetics are those who practice hatha-yoga, another part of the Hindu religion. They have learned how to control their bodies in quite marvelous ways. In addition to positioning themselves in strange postures, they are able to regulate their breathing and to exist in yogi-sleep, a state in which their respiration and pulse rates are slowed and they can be buried alive for several days. These ascetics claim that they use their minds to withdraw from life as we know it and, as a result, become insensitive to heat, cold, or pain.

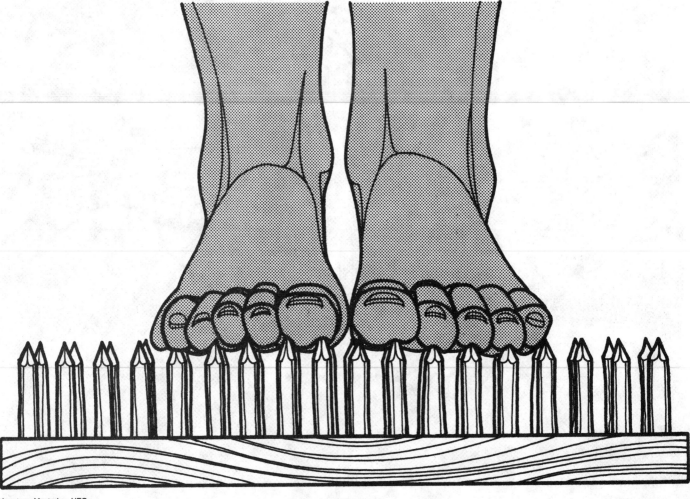

People Without Pain Activity Sheet

▲ 1. Construct a shoe box diorama showing a fakir walking barefoot on nails.

■ 2. Interview a hypnotist to find out how it is possible for a person not to feel cold, heat, or pain while hypnotized. Report your findings.

▲ 3. Draw a map of Asia. On it show the locations of the major religious groups—Buddhist, Confucian, Hindu, and Muslim.

■ 4. Write a story about a fakir who becomes known as a "faker."

■ 5. Design a collage showing the many skills mastered by fakirs.

◉ 6. Tell why you do or do not believe anyone could walk barefoot on hot coals.

Name _____

The Mystery of Excalibur

Historians have long argued whether King Arthur was real or legendary. According to the historical view, Arthur probably lived during the sixth century and was a military leader or king of the Britons. Most scholars believe that he was not a king but a person of great national importance.

The legendary view of Arthur calls him *dux bellorum*, or leader of battle. Arthur carried a very special weapon, a sword with a jeweled hilt and magic powers. This sword was called Excalibur.

There are many legends about Arthur's marvelous sword. One legend says that a magician named Merlin set the sword in stone. This sword could only be removed by a future king. Arthur removed that sword while still a young boy. Another legend says that Arthur came upon the Lady of the Lake, who gave him the sword. The sword was kept in a scabbard, which had the power to keep its wearer free from losing any blood, even if mortally wounded.

Arthur was supposed to have been leader of the Knights of the Round Table. Legend says that Arthur and his knights led the Celts against the Anglo-Saxons and that, in the final battle at Mount Badon, Arthur single-handedly killed 960 men.

At the end of Arthur's life, it is said that he (or possibly one of his knights) threw Excalibur into the lake, where it was grasped by a reaching hand.

In 1191, monks at the Glastonbury Abbey in Southwest England claimed to have discovered the bodies of King Arthur and his wife, Guinevere. Truth or myth? Recently discovered historical documents may give us the answer.

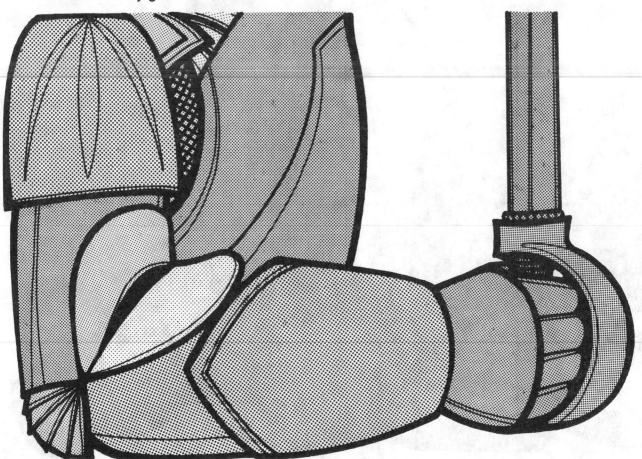

Name _____

Excalibur Activity Sheet

1. Design a game based on the legendary exploits of King Arthur.

2. Illustrate in detail Arthur's receiving Excalibur from the Lady of the Lake.

3. Read about King Arthur in *Le Morte d'Arthur,* compiled and translated by Sir Thomas Malory.

4. Create a new legend about King Arthur. In this legend, assign even greater and more wonderful powers to Excalibur.

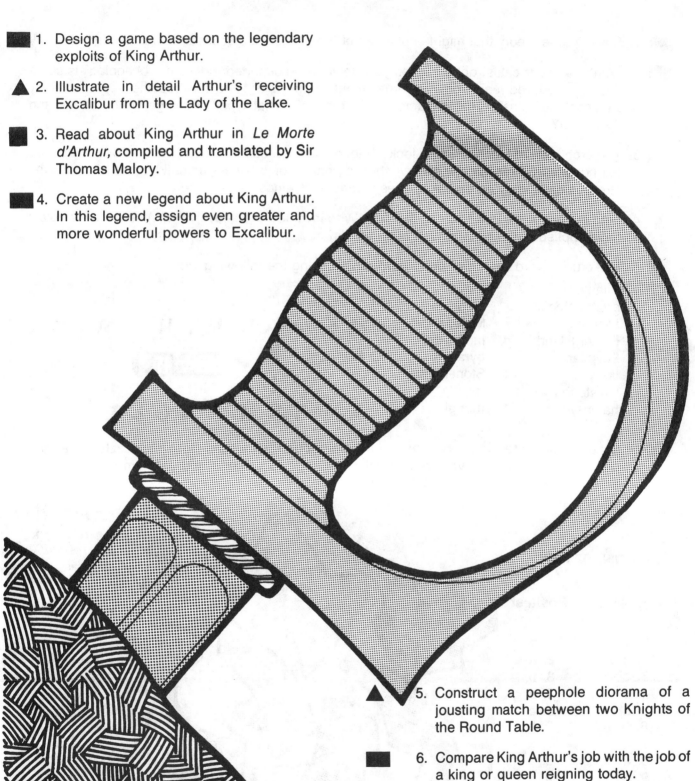

5. Construct a peephole diorama of a jousting match between two Knights of the Round Table.

6. Compare King Arthur's job with the job of a king or queen reigning today.

7. Tell why you do or do not believe that Arthur, as king, was really the leader of the Knights of the Round Table.

Correlated Activities

■ 1. Develop one theory that might explain all of the mysteries discussed in this section.

■ 2. What if a major catastrophe caused your town to be deserted today? If archaeologists came back five hundred years from now, what might they be able to find out about the way you lived by studying the ruins? What artifacts would remain? What types of things would decay and disappear?

■ 3. The architects of Machu Picchu locked stones together so that their buildings could withstand earthquakes. Do research to discover how architects of today design buildings to withstand the stresses caused by earthquakes, fires, floods, and winds.

▲ 4. Find out about the Pythagorean theorem. Who invented or discovered it? When? How would it have applied to the construction of pyramids?

● 5. Make up a word search or crossword puzzle using the following words:

■
Atlantis	Maya
archaeologist	megalith
ascetic	Minoan
Easter Island	monolith
Egyptian	pyramid
fakir	Stonehenge
Glastonbury	temple
hatha-yoga	triangle

■ 6. Draw a picture of a large pot that might have been found at Knossos. Cut it into puzzle pieces and put the pieces in an envelope. Hand the envelope to a friend and ask him or her to play archaeologist and put the pot back together.

Answer Key

Pretest	Posttest
1. c	1. b
2. a	2. a
3. c	3. b
4. b	4. a
5. a	5. c
6. b	6. b
7. a	7. a
8. a	8. a
9. c	9. c
10. b	10. c

Name _____

Posttest

Circle the letter beside the answer that best completes each sentence.

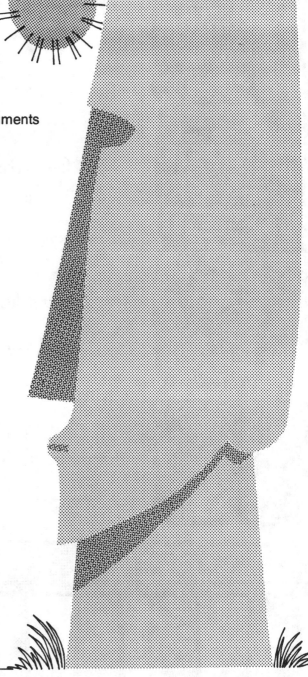

1. The lost continent of Atlantis might have been located
   a. in the South Pacific.
   b. in the Mediterranean Sea.
   c. near Antarctica.

2. Huge stone heads were found
   a. on Easter Island.
   b. with the pyramids.
   c. at Stonehenge.

3. It is amazing that early people could build monuments
   a. without leaders.
   b. without iron tools.
   c. without large numbers of workers.

4. The island of Crete was settled by the
   a. Minoans.
   b. Mycenaeans.
   c. Maya.

5. Crete might have been part of
   a. the Round Table.
   b. the Devil's Triangle.
   c. Atlantis.

6. Stonehenge was probably built as a huge
   a. temple.
   b. astronomical calendar.
   c. landing field.

7. Nazca is the location of
   a. earth etchings and lines.
   b. huge archaeological mounds.
   c. the pyramid of Cheops.

8. The Indus Valley is like Easter Island in its
   a. hieroglyphics.
   b. stone figures.
   c. temples.

9. A fakir and a yogi are both
   a. leaders of early tribes.
   b. Minoan priests.
   c. ascetics.

10. Excalibur was a well-known
    a. active volcano.
    b. ancient city.
    c. wondrous weapon.

This is
to certify that

_____
(name of student)

has successfully completed
a unit of study
on

Mysteries

and has been named a

Mystery Sleuth

in recognition of this accomplishment.

_____
(signature of teacher)

_____
(date)

Bulletin Board Ideas

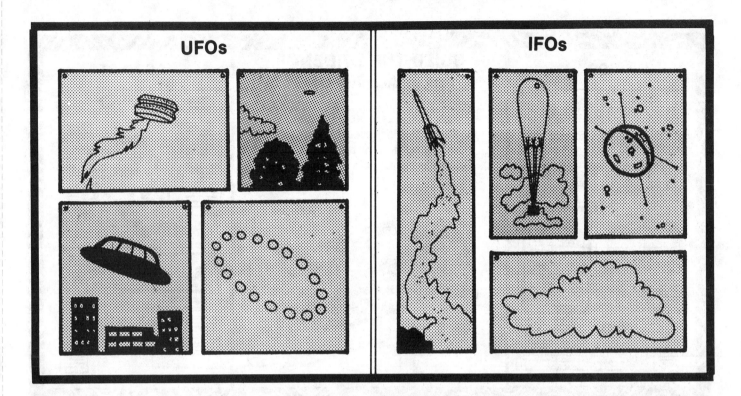

UFOs

IFOs

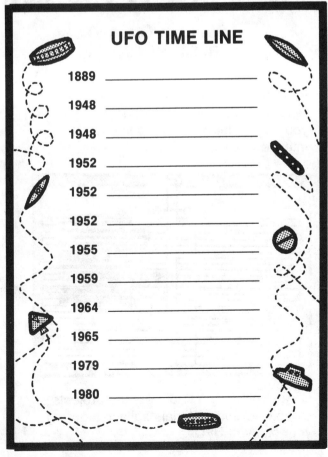

UFO TIME LINE

1889 _____

1948 _____

1948 _____

1952 _____

1952 _____

1952 _____

1955 _____

1959 _____

1964 _____

1965 _____

1979 _____

1980 _____

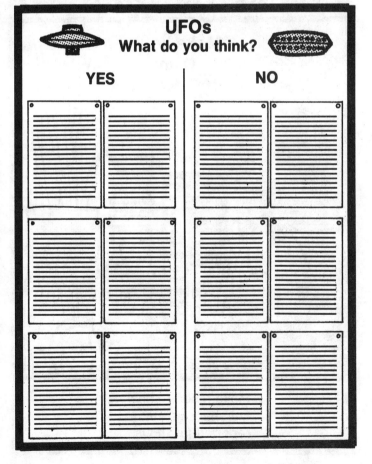

UFOs
What do you think?

YES   NO

Learning Center Ideas

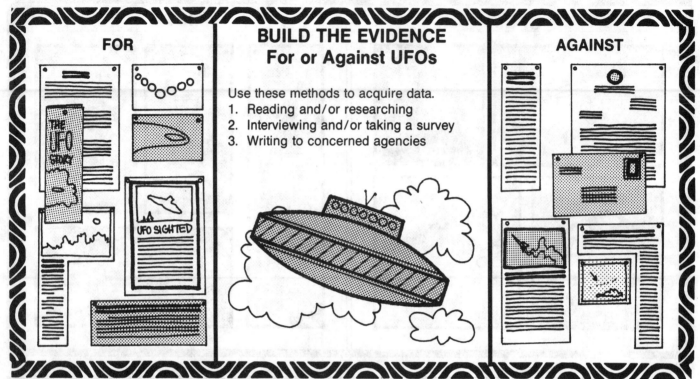

FOR

BUILD THE EVIDENCE
For or Against UFOs

Use these methods to acquire data.
1. Reading and/or researching
2. Interviewing and/or taking a survey
3. Writing to concerned agencies

AGAINST

Make Your Own UFO Model

Make models showing the shapes usually reported for UFOs.

Set up a Class BLUE BOOK

In a notebook, put together all of the UFO reports you've read about and any more you can acquire through personal interviews.

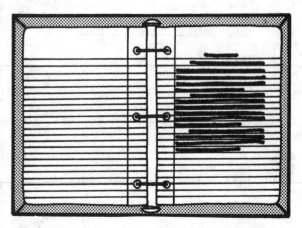

Create a museum to display the projects completed and materials collected during your study of UFOs.

Name _____

Pretest

The following questions are either true or false. If a question is **true**, write a **T** on the line in front of it. If a question is **false**, write an **F** on the line in front of it.

___ 1. Barney and Betty Hill say that they were taken to Venus by a UFO.

___ 2. A president of the United States reported sighting a UFO.

___ 3. Astronomers know that UFOs are not real.

___ 4. Some people confuse Venus with a UFO.

___ 5. UFOs were seen in California during the 1800s.

___ 6. The Gallup Poll is for counting horses, ships, and UFOs.

___ 7. Many UFOs are shaped like cigars.

___ 8. Lightning can form a ball and bounce along the ground.

___ 9. Very few Americans really believe in the existence of UFOs.

___ 10. IFOs are illuminated flying objects.

___ 11. A hoax is an act intended to trick someone.

___ 12. Members of the air force study UFOs because they believe these objects exist and want to protect us from them.

___ 13. Some people believe that UFOs come from a civilization beneath the ocean.

___ 14. Many UFOs are easily explained or identified.

___ 15. Most UFOs are not identified because they are secret weapons of the United States or other nations.

___ 16. Pilots have chased UFOs that turned out to be balloons.

___ 17. Some UFOs are really meteors.

___ 18. Pilots have reported seeing double-decked spaceships.

___ 19. Many people have been ridiculed because they reported sighting UFOs.

___ 20. There have been no cases of radiation exposure associated with UFO sightings.

Name _____

UFO or IFO?

UFO is an abbreviation or acronym for unidentified flying object. UFOs have been reported for centuries but not really in great numbers until the second half of the twentieth century. Since we have entered the air and space age, many objects have been put into the sky. Some of these objects have been misidentified and have been considered UFOs by observers only until experts have figured out what they were. Most UFOs are explained and then become IFOs (identified flying objects). Some, however, are never identified, and therein lies the mystery.

Where did these objects come from? Many guesses have been made. Skeptics say they are figments of the imagination. Believers say they are spaceships from far out in our galaxy or even beyond. Others suggest that they may come from a planet within our own solar system. There are even those who say that these spaceships come from our planet, from a civilization under the sea.

Are these objects manned by living beings? Many people believe that UFOs, if they really exist, are only unmanned probes sent here to investigate this planet in the same way we send satellites and space probes to investigate other planets in our solar system.

How did these objects get here? If they came from under the ocean, they originated here. If they originated elsewhere, they could have come accidentally, drifting off course, or they might have been deliberately sent to this planet.

What might be the purpose of their coming? They might be lost or in need of help. Or, perhaps they have come as scientific explorers or as military spies. They might even be colonists searching for a new home.

Whatever UFOs are or are not, it is fun to speculate about them.

Name _____

UFO Investigation

In the United States, there are two organizations whose sole purpose is to study, identify, and classify UFOs. The official government organization is the air force. In 1948, air force UFO specialists used the code name Sign, which was later changed to Grudge. In 1952, the name was again changed, this time to Project Blue Book, and its employees were stationed at the Aerospace Technical Intelligence Center, more commonly called ATIC. It was located at Wright-Patterson Air Force Base in Ohio. Project Blue Book was disbanded in 1969, and now NASA handles UFO inquiries.

Those in charge of Project Blue Book did not come up with explanations for all UFO sightings, but their basic philosophy was that UFOs were probably misinterpretations of identifiable objects (planes, missiles, balloons, satellites, and the like), meteorological phenomena, hoaxes, or the hallucinations of crazy people. Because there had never been any concrete evidence to prove that "flying saucers" existed, Project Blue Book employees assumed that they did not.

The second investigative group, made up of scientists, aviators, engineers, and others, is the National Investigation Commission on Aerial Phenomena (NICAP), which was formed in 1956. Members of this private group try to do three things. First, they investigate all UFO reports. Second, they try to discover and expose hoaxes and irresponsible reports. Third, they publicize data from reliable sources such as pilots and scientists. The NICAP philosophy is that UFOs may exist and could be from outer space.

Because of their different philosophies, these two organizations often investigate the same reported UFO sightings and come to totally opposite conclusions. Is it any wonder, then, that the average citizen doesn't know what to believe?

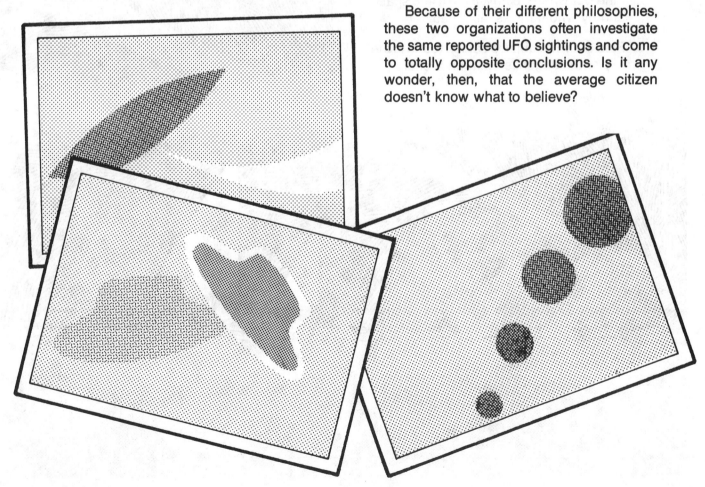

Name _____

Death of a Satellite

Sometimes UFO sightings are very easily explained. Shortly after midnight on April 8, 1964, residents in Connecticut reported seeing a very bright blue-white light traveling at a super speed. Some even reported seeing its color change to red. Smaller pieces seemed to come out and trail behind. All along the eastern seaboard, people called radio stations and police departments to report many and varied sightings. Soon ships in the Caribbean were reporting in. By the time the object reached the Virgin Islands, it had turned green with an orange streak. People in British Guiana who saw it reported a red object that disappeared into the Atlantic Ocean.

In tracking down the reports, an alert reporter realized that the object had to have traveled in a straight line from north to south, covering the total distance in five minutes. That would be a speed of 16,000 miles per hour. No airplane could travel that fast! The incident was quickly explained, however, when the world learned that *Sputnik II* had plunged to earth at that time.

The same kinds of observations were made on March 7, 1960, when a fiery object was visible from Lake Erie to Miami, Florida. It was later identified as the satellite, *Discovery VIII,* breaking up.

Activities

1. Draw a map of the area involved and trace the route of *Sputnik II.*

2. Find out when *Sputnik II* went into space and by whom it was launched.

3. Find out what objects can be found in the sky and categorize them on a chart.

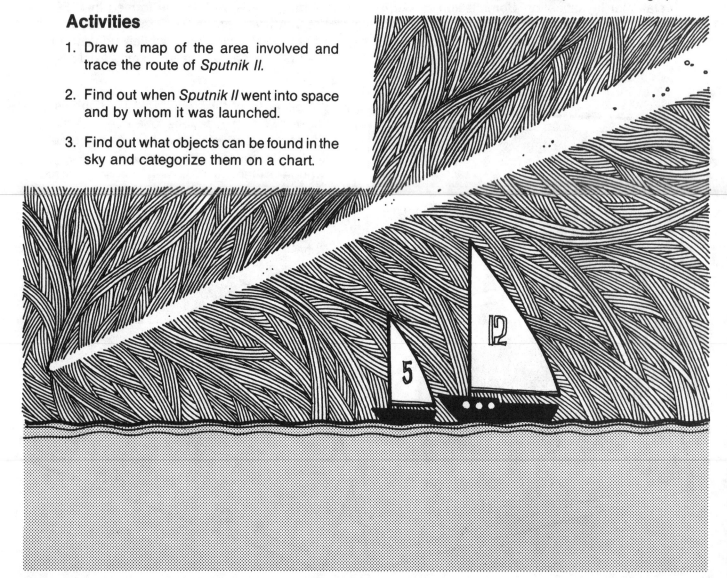

Name _____

Ball Lightning

One explanation for a number of UFO reports may be ball lightning. Ball lightning, also called *Kugelblitz,* is a rarely seen phenomenon that looks like a ball of fire, can move along slowly, and can disappear noisily or quietly.

For many years, few people believed in ball lightning, but those who had seen it were firmly convinced. One housewife, for example, had a ball of lightning drop down her chimney and into her kitchen. As she ran from the room, it followed her and then moved out the door, across the yard, and into the barn, where it exploded, burning the barn down.

In 1966, Westinghouse reported that two of its scientists might have an explanation for this strange phenomenon. They theorized that when a ball of air warmer than the air surrounding it became charged with electricity, it would light up. They put numbers representing these conditions into a computer. The computer output confirmed that those conditions would produce a grapefruit-sized object that would light up and glow with the brightness of a 1,000-watt bulb. This size and brightness match eyewitness descriptions of ball lightning exactly. These scientists also found that this ball of lightning would move and could disappear silently or with a bang.

Because many UFOs act in the manner described for ball lightning, this electrical phenomenon may account for some of the still unidentified flying objects.

Activities

1. Find out about Benjamin Franklin's theories of lightning and the methods he used to test them. Share what you learn with the class.

2. Write a story about a boy or girl who has an exciting encounter with ball lightning.

Name _____

Early Vision

One of the earliest recorded UFO sightings took place in Sacramento, California, on Tuesday, November 17, 1889. That afternoon many subscribers to the local paper, the *Sacramento Bee,* read an article which stated that someone would arrive from the East in two days by air. Because the airplane had not yet been successfully flown, the statement was ridiculous and was probably dismissed as such by most of those who read it.

Later that evening, however, "hundreds" of people on the streets of Sacramento saw an "electric arc lamp propelled by some mysterious force" gliding in and out among the rooftops. The lamp reportedly moved from fifty to two thousand feet above the ground and was cigar- or oval-shaped with winglike propellers or wheels turning very fast. There was a dark mass on its top and a strong light at the bottom, and some observers even said that there was a four-man crew singing, laughing, and shouting inside the craft.

Residents of Sacramento were not the only ones who witnessed this amazing sight. Four days later, the same object appeared in San Francisco, sailing "against the wind." Everyone knew it could not possibly be a balloon. Many so-called reliable witnesses acknowledged that they had seen the aircraft but later disavowed the sightings because they feared they would be ridiculed.

As time went on, stories about the mysterious aircraft became even wilder. One man said that the craft had landed on his property. Another man, an electrician, said that it had stopped and picked him up to make repairs.

Name _____

Early Vision Activity Sheet

1. Pretend that you are a reporter for the *Sacramento Bee.* Write a factual account of the mysterious sightings. Remember to tell who, what, when, why, and where.

2. How fast would the mysterious craft have been traveling if it took four days to go directly from Sacramento to San Francisco?

3. If a traveler in 1889 were traveling from New York to Sacramento, what modes of transportation would he or she be most likely to use and how long would each take?

4. Compare the description and drawing of the UFO on page 84 with descriptions of UFOs seen during this century. In what ways are they alike? In what ways are they different?

The Sacramento Bee

Name _____

The Mantell Search

One famous UFO incident was that of Captain Thomas Mantell. On January 7, 1948, switchboards lighted up at the Kentucky State Highway Patrol Office in Frankfort, Kentucky. People were calling to report the sighting of a strange object in the sky. Some observers said that the huge object was three hundred feet in diameter. Its flight path seemed to be taking it toward Fort Knox, which is where the United States stores its gold, so the highway patrol officers decided to let personnel at Godman Air Force Base know about the UFO's existence.

National guard planes in the area were contacted, and Flight Leader Thomas Mantell agreed to take a look. He and two of the planes under his command went out to intercept the object.

Captain Mantell and his fellow pilots spotted the object and began to chase it. They described it as being metallic, of tremendous size, and shaped like a teardrop. The three planes pursued the mysterious craft for awhile. Then two of them ran short of fuel and had to return to the base. Captain Mantell continued the chase alone. For a short time, radio contact with Mantell was lost. When his voice was heard again, he said that he was following the object, which was moving at his speed or better, and that he would close in for a better look. Even though he had no oxygen mask, he went up to an elevation of 25,000 feet.

Unfortunately, Captain Mantell's plane crashed. There were no burns and no radiation. Even though there were wild rumors that he had been attacked by men from outer space, it became evident that he had flown too high, had lost consciousness, and had gone into a dive.

At first the government said the object Mantell had spotted and mistakenly followed was probably Venus. But UFO enthusiasts said, "No!" Later the government reluctantly admitted that Captain Mantell had been chasing a Skyhook balloon, part of a secret government project.

Name _____

The Mantell Search Activity Sheet

1. It was five years before the United States government reluctantly admitted that Captain Mantell was probably chasing a Skyhook balloon. On a separate piece of paper, write a paragraph explaining why it took so long.

2. Do research to discover the purpose of the Skyhook balloons. Then share your findings with the class.

3. Write a creative story in which an alien aircraft of some kind is used to steal the gold stored at Fort Knox.

4. Make a picture chart on which different kinds of weather balloons are illustrated, identified, and briefly described.

Name _____

The Sutton Events

Two interesting events, both involving the name Sutton and menacing space creatures, occurred during the 1950s. The first took place in 1952 near Sutton, West Virginia. A woman, her three sons, and a seventeen-year-old boy saw something strange land near their home. When they went to investigate, they were first aware of a horrible odor. Next they saw two eyes shining in the glow of their flashlight. Finally they saw a nine-foot-tall creature with a monstrous face. The creature made a hissing sound.

Frightened, the woman and boys ran home. Once there, the mother noticed an oily film on her sons' faces. Because their throats had begun to swell, she called a doctor. When he examined the boys, he found that their throats were inflamed as if they had come in contact with mustard gas.

By the time the sheriff arrived at the home, the weather was foggy and he could see nothing. When he took his hounds to the scene of the strange encounter, they ran off howling. The next morning, the sheriff received a call from a man who said he had just seen a strange object leaving the hill. Again, nothing could be found upon investigation.

This incident was never investigated by air force officers, because they felt it was not a valid sighting. Many of the lady's neighbors believed that she was telling the truth, but nothing could be proved.

The second event took place in Kentucky in 1955, and involved a family named Sutton. The Suttons were entertaining some friends when they heard their dogs barking. They went to investigate and saw a glowing creature. The men got their guns, ran outside, and shot at the creature. They reported hearing at least one shot ricochet as if it had struck some kind of metal. They ran back into the house, turned off the lights, and told everyone to take cover.

Later, when the men turned on a light, they saw a helmeted creature peering in the window. They shot at the creature, breaking the glass and causing the creature to fall back. They went outside to have a look. There they saw two more creatures, one in a tree and one on the rooftop, and shot at both. Again they returned to the house. They hid in the dark for two hours before going for help. (They had no telephone.)

When investigators arrived, they found the broken window but no other evidence to prove or disprove the story.

Name _____

The Sutton Events Activity Sheet

1. If you had been the director of Project Blue Book, would you have sent a team to investigate the Sutton, West Virginia, incident? Why or why not?

2. What characteristics do the two Sutton events have in common?

3. Find out more about mustard gas. Where does it come from? What is its chemical composition? How is it made? What effects does it have on people? How is it used? Share your findings with the class.

4. Draw a picture of the creatures the people in West Virginia and in Kentucky might have seen.

Name _____

The Missing Scoutmaster

In 1952, in West Palm Beach, Florida, a scoutmaster offered to drive some scouts home after a meeting. On the way, the group discussed a number of topics, especially things that scared them. The scoutmaster mentioned unidentified flying objects, and all of the boys agreed that an encounter with a UFO would be scary.

The boys continued to talk among themselves while the scoutmaster concentrated on the dark, deserted country road. Suddenly he pulled to one side and parked the car. He explained that he had just seen some strange lights in the trees, which was odd because there were no houses in the vicinity. When the lights appeared again, the scoutmaster announced he was going to investigate. He grabbed two flashlights and a machete. He told the boys to stay in the car and, if he did not return in fifteen minutes, to go for help.

After waiting for what seemed a very long time, the boys finally agreed to go as a group for help. They ran down the road until they came to a house. They knocked on the door, asked to use the phone, and called the sheriff. When the sheriff arrived, the boys led him back to the car. The scoutmaster was nowhere to be seen, so the sheriff and his deputy decided to go into the woods to look for him. Rather than staying alone in the car, the boys went along.

As before, the woods were dark, and it was hard to see anything. Soon, though, the sheriff, his deputy, and the boys heard a moan. Moving toward it, they found the scoutmaster struggling to get up. He seemed quite frantic and wanted to know if "they" were gone yet. He said that when he had gone into the woods he had noticed a terrible odor and that it had gotten very hot. Then a huge object had hovered over him, sending down a ball of fire which caught him in its licking flames. At that point, he sheepishly admitted, he had fainted and could tell no more of what had happened. All he knew was that the back of one of his hands had been singed and that a hole had been burned in his hat. Because nothing more could be done at that late hour, the sheriff and his deputy took the scouts home, and the scoutmaster went on his own way.

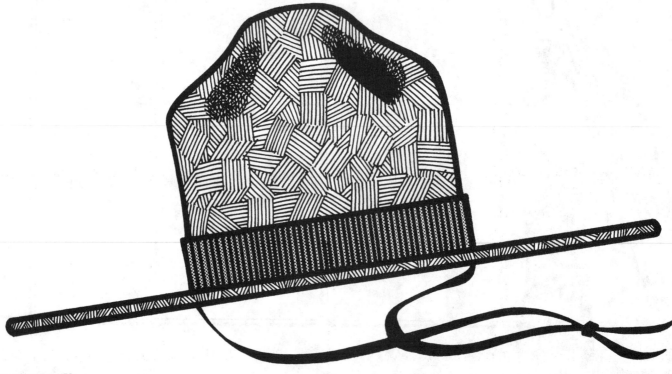

Name _____

The Missing Scoutmaster
(continued)

When Project Blue Book heard about the incident a couple of days later, they sent Captain Edward J. Ruppelt to find out more about it. Ruppelt questioned the sheriff, who assured the captain that his part of the story was correct. Then Ruppelt talked with the scoutmaster. The scoutmaster told Ruppelt that he had gone to a military academy, had served in the armed forces in World War II, and then had run a gas station until becoming a clerk in a hardware store; but he refused to say anything about what he had seen because he had hired a press agent and was going to sell his story.

When Captain Ruppelt tried to check the scoutmaster's story, he found a lot of discrepancies. The scoutmaster had never been in the war. In fact, he had been dishonorably discharged from the marines. He had served time in jail and had been fired from his job at the gas station. When investigators checked the exact spot where the lights were first seen, they too saw lights flickering through the trees and quickly identified them as the lights of planes landing at the local airport.

Based on this information, it was decided that the whole incident was a hoax—one that scared a lot of people, cost the government a great deal of money to investigate, and caused everyone to be more skeptical about UFO reports.

Activities

1. Create a dramatization of this incident and present it to your class.

2. Imagine what might have happened if the boys had gone into the woods instead of going for help. Write an account describing how that might have changed the hoax.

3. Draw a cartoon strip illustrating the events in this story.

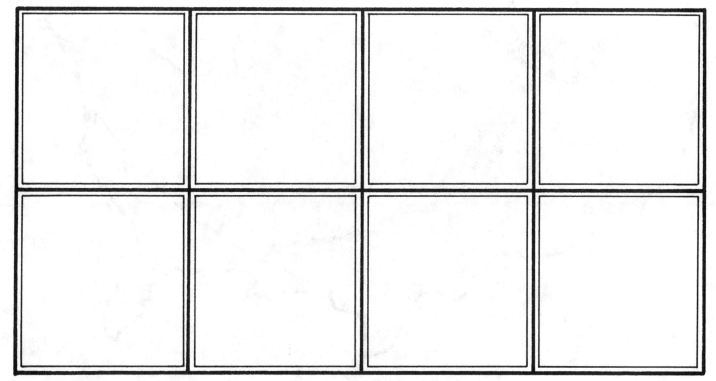

Name _____

Pilot Reports

The air force and most commercial airline companies have asked their pilots and flight personnel not to report unusual sightings to the public, but over the years some very interesting incidents have come to light. One of these occurred on July 24, 1948, when an Eastern Airlines DC-3 was flying from Houston, Texas, to Boston, Massachusetts. The pilot, Captain Clarence S. Chiles, was an experienced airman with more than 8,500 flying hours and was accompanied by an equally experienced first officer. Near Montgomery, Alabama, they noticed a bright light approaching them from straight in front. It was moving so fast that it could not be a plane. To avoid a head-on collision, the pilot made a sharp left turn. The light zipped by less than seven hundred feet from the plane.

Both the pilot and the first officer had seen exactly the same thing. They described it as a "double-decked" spaceship. They said that its double rows of windows gave off a bluish-white light, and that it left behind a fifty-foot trail of orange-red flame. When they radioed their information to the control tower, they were told that there were no other aircraft in the area.

Because this was in the early days of UFO reports, everyone was very skeptical. Air force spokesmen said that the pilot and his first officer had seen a shooting star. Chiles had seen many shooting stars and knew that this was something different, but he was never able to change the official record because he had no proof. As a result, many pilots became hesitant to report UFO sightings for fear of being ignored or, worse yet, ridiculed.

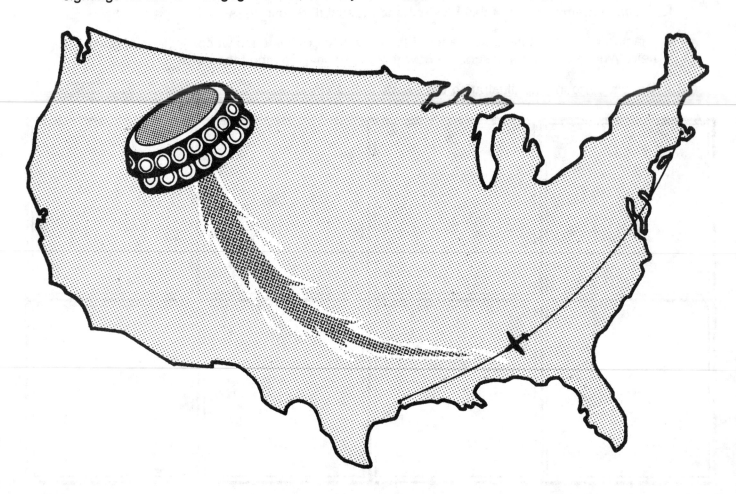

Name _____

Pilot Reports Activity Sheet

▲ 1. Make a papier mâché model of a double-decked spaceship.

■ 2. Design a plan for the interior of a double-decked, pancake- or hat-shaped spaceship.

■ 3. If you were Captain Chiles and had to write an official account of the sighting, what would you say?

◉ 4. Do you believe Captain Chiles and his first officer really saw a double-decked spaceship? Why or why not?

■ 5. If you saw a spaceship tonight, what would you do about it? How would you check to be sure about what you saw? Whom would you tell? What specific details would you observe and include in your report to make it more believable?

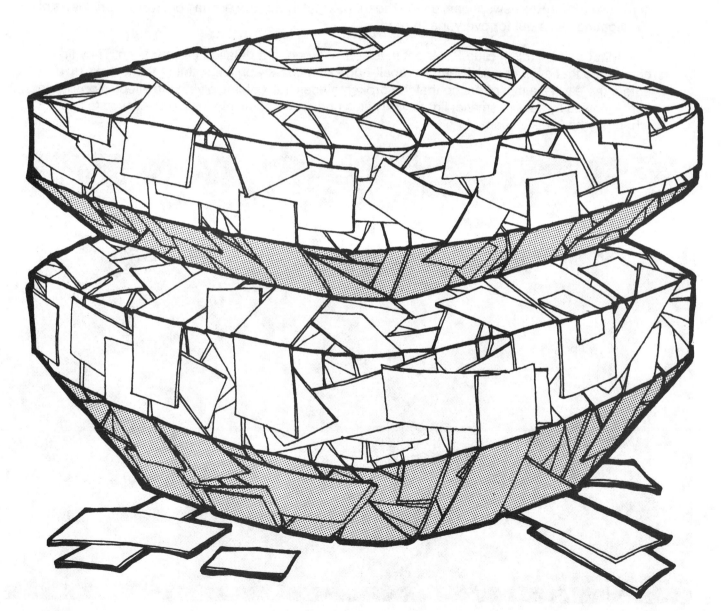

Name _____

Flight 947

At 3:00 a.m. Hawaii time on July 12, 1959, American Airways Flight 947 was over the Pacific Ocean enroute from San Francisco to Honolulu. The trip was strictly routine until Captain C. A. Wilson sighted a cluster of five white lights—one big light and four smaller ones. The lights headed straight toward his airliner at a fantastic rate of speed, then veered sharply to the right and disappeared. Captain Wilson immediately reported what he had seen to the control center, as did the crewmen aboard nine other planes in the vicinity. Although each man reported in a calm voice, it was evident to the air traffic controller that all of them had seen something very unusual.

Upon arrival at the airport in Honolulu, Captain Wilson and his crew, along with others who had seen the strange light formation, were interviewed by military intelligence officers with some reporters in attendance. They were asked to describe again what they had seen. One reporter even asked if they might have seen a flying saucer. Captain Wilson replied that he had never before believed in flying saucers, "but," he added, "I'm a believer now." The others in the room agreed with him. The next day the newspapers carried headlines that flying saucers had been seen, and news of the sightings was out for everyone to read.

At that point, Project Blue Book got involved and began a detailed investigation. They finally concluded that everyone had seen a fireball—an exceptionally brilliant meteor that breaks up as it enters the earth's atmosphere so that the broken pieces trail behind, giving the effect of one large light followed by several smaller lights. The pilots and crews of the planes were relieved to find out what they had really seen!

Name _____

Flight 947 Activity Sheet

1. Write and produce a skit in which the events experienced by crewmen aboard American Airlines Flight 947 are reenacted.

2. Make a flip book that shows the movement of lights toward Flight 947 and then their veering off to the right.

3. Pretend that you are a reporter assigned to interview Captain Wilson. On the lines below, list ten specific questions you plan to ask him.

1. _____

2. _____

3. _____

4. _____

5. _____

6. _____

7. _____

8. _____

9. _____

10. _____

4. Do research to find out about meteors and fireballs. Share what you learn with the class.

Name _____

The Mystery Blips

One of the most mysterious of all pilot sightings occurred on December 6, 1952, when a B-29 bomber was flying over the Gulf of Mexico. It was a beautiful, clear night. Suddenly, the bomber's radar picked up a blip moving at a speed the flight engineer figured to be in excess of 5,000 miles per hour. Shortly thereafter, a second blip appeared on the screen. Then there were four, all directly ahead. Suddenly one blip veered to the right, and all of the blips vanished from the screen. Less than three minutes later, the blips were back, traveling at the same fantastic speed and heading toward the plane on a collision course. At the last minute, they veered to the right again. A brightly lighted objected flashed by, and then all blips vanished from the screen.

Six minutes later, all four blips were back on the screen. The only difference was that two blue-white lights flashed by the plane. Seconds later, five blips appeared. At first, the blips were moving crosswise to the plane, but then they swerved and headed straight for it. Before the pilot could even react, the blips just stopped and then began to trail the bomber! Ten seconds later, a huge blip, double the size of the others, appeared on the screen. The other four blips moved over and merged with the big blip, which then flashed brightly and left the radar screen entirely.

When the plane landed, all of the crew members were closely interrogated by intelligence officers from a nearby base, and all told the same story. The intelligence officers asked if the pilot and crew members really had seen a mother ship take off with the other UFOs. All stated that they had never said that—they had merely seen four or five smaller blips merge with one large blip.

This sighting was investigated further by Project Blue Book, but the evidence was inconclusive. The case was finally marked "unexplained."

Name _____

The Mystery Blips Activity Sheet

1. Find out what radar is, how it works, and what blips are.

2. Why were the pilots unwilling to admit that they might have seen a large mother ship controlling the smaller UFOs? Explain your answer.

3. In what ways do the details in this story resemble the reports given by crewmen aboard Flight 947? In what ways are they different?

4. Make up a story to explain what the blips were and why they were there.

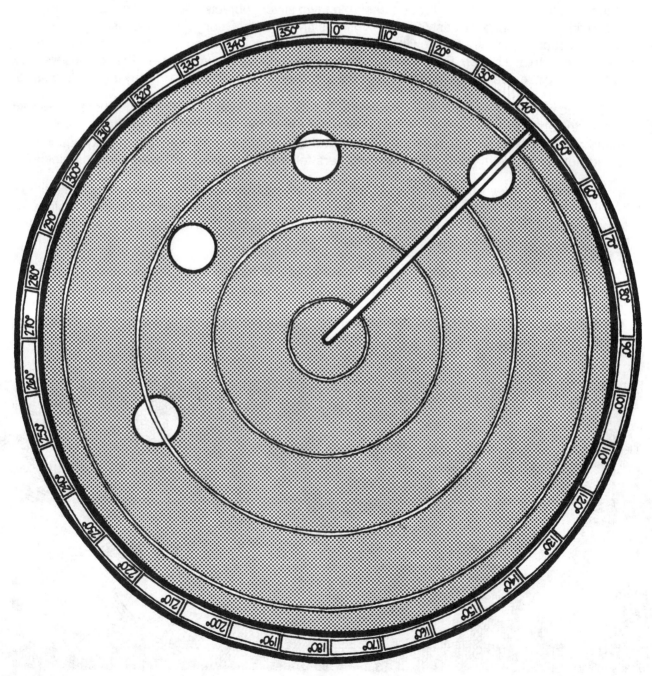

Name _____

Astronomers and Astronauts

Some of the people who have reported seeing UFOs have been highly respected scientists, astronomers, and astronauts. One of them was Clyde Tombaugh, the American astronomer who discovered Pluto in 1930. His experience with a UFO occurred in 1949 while he was working at the White Sands Missile Range in New Mexico. Tombaugh and his wife saw two rows of parallel lights that passed silently by. The lights were yellow-green in color, like nothing Tombaugh had ever seen before, and left the astronomer petrified and totally amazed.

Tombaugh was not the first astronomer to have such an experience. In 1883, Mexican astronomer José Bonilla observed and photographed four hundred objects moving across the face of the sun. In 1954, a British astronomer sighted two silvery objects and a third gray, oval object—each with a diameter of at least 50 feet—while visiting Atlanta, Georgia. In 1955, astronomer Frank Halstead spent eight minutes viewing a cigar-shaped object followed by a disc-shaped object in California's Mojave Desert. French astronomer Jacques Chapuis, working at a French observatory in 1957, reported seeing a yellow, starlike object that went straight up into the sky and disappeared.

To find out how many scientists had really sighted some kind of UFO, Stanford astrophysicist Peter Sturrock took a survey of the 2,611-member American Astronomical Society in 1975. More than half responded with sixty-two reporting that they had seen an object in the sky which they could not identify. A majority of the astronomers felt that UFOs should be studied scientifically.

The crew of *Apollo 11* reported that their capsule was "paced by what seemed to be a mass of intelligent energy." Astronauts who participated in the Gemini, Apollo, and Skylab missions all reported sighting unidentifiable objects. According to one report, the Pentagon has admitted that it may have had telepathic contact with UFOs.

Even a former president of the United States admits to having once seen something in the sky that he and his companions at the time could not identify. The sighting took place in 1969 and was not reported until 1973. Some have said that the group probably saw only Venus, but others feel that the president, Jimmy Carter, a navy veteran with extensive navigational experience, would not have made that kind of error.

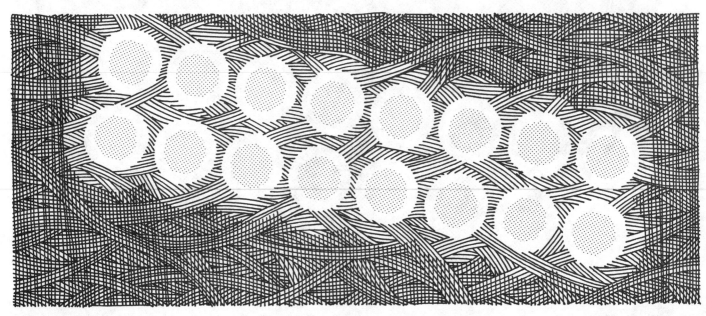

Name _____

Astronomers and Astronauts Activity Sheet

1. Interview an astronomer or scientist from your town to find out how he or she feels about UFOs. Share your findings with the class.

2. Find out what kind of sightings were made by astronauts taking part in the Gemini and Skylab missions. Share what you learn.

3. Write a more detailed description of a "mass of intelligent energy." What might it look like? Where might it come from? How might it move?

4. Using a telescope, locate five objects in the sky and learn to identify them.

5. Why did Jimmy Carter wait four years before reporting the sighting of a UFO? Give several possible reasons. Choose the one reason you think is most plausible. Then explain why you chose it.

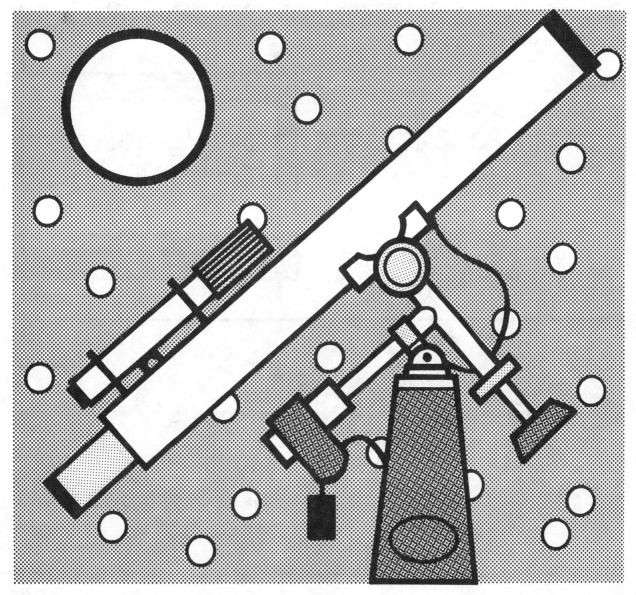

Name _____

The Exeter Event

On September 3, 1965, Norman Muscarello, a teen-ager who lived in Exeter, New Hampshire, was hitchhiking home at two o'clock in the morning. The air was clear, and visibility was good despite the darkness. Suddenly, Norman saw a large object surrounded by flashing lights. Without a sound, the object began to move toward him with a tipping motion. Norman, who thought it was going to hit him, dove into a gully next to the road. The object came forward, hovered over him, and then moved silently away.

Norman got up and ran to a nearby house screaming for help. No one was home, but just then a car pulled into the driveway. Norman pleaded with the occupants to take him to the police, which they did. At first, the police did not believe Norman's story; but after a second person reported seeing exactly the same thing, a policeman was dispatched to the scene with Norman. There they and a second patrolman who arrived soon all saw the mysterious object.

During the next few weeks, many reports of sightings were made. At first, the air force explained them in terms of unusual weather phenomena. Later, no clear explanation was offered. To this day, Norman Muscarello and some of the other citizens of Exeter will gladly tell you about their personal experiences with a "flying saucer."

Activities

1. Retell the story by illustrating it on a roll of paper and "showing" it in a box with an opening cut to resemble a television screen.

2. Do research to find out more about the other sightings in Exeter in 1965 and 1966. Share your findings with the class.

3. Describe how you would have felt if you had been in Norman's shoes.

Name _____

Human Observation

All UFO reports are based on human observation, which is subject to distortion and error. To understand how eyewitnesses can give differing or inaccurate accounts, show this picture to five people, one at a time. Allow each person to study the picture for fifteen seconds. Then cover it and ask your subject to describe the scene to you. Either tape record or write down the descriptions. Compare them, and use them to draw some conclusions about human observation.

Name _____

The Lost Hours

One of the most amazing UFO stories of all began on September 19, 1961, when a New Hampshire couple, Barney and Betty Hill, were driving home from a brief vacation in Canada. Because they were running short of cash, they decided to drive on through to their home instead of staying one more night in a motel. At approximately ten o'clock, they stopped for a bite to eat. Barney figured the rest of the drive would take about four and one-half hours. They would be home before three o'clock in the morning.

They took a dark, deserted route through the mountains. Suddenly, they spied a very bright light. At first they thought it was a star. Then they decided it was a satellite. As it got closer and larger, they decided it was a plane. The only problem was that it made no sound.

When the object neared the ground, the Hills stopped beside the road to get a better view. Finally, Barney got out of the car with a pair of binoculars. The object was less than one thousand feet away. Even though he was scared, curiosity got the best of Barney, and he moved closer to it. What he saw in his binoculars was beyond belief! There, in front of him, was a pancake-shaped object hovering over the ground. Inside its bright windows could be seen several figures working at the controls. From their movements, Barney concluded that one of the figures was the leader.

At that point, Barney went running back to the car, and the object lifted higher into the air. Shortly thereafter, Barney heard several beeps from the rear of his car and began to feel sleepy. When he recovered from his sleepiness, he heard several more beeps and realized that he wasn't far from home.

Upon returning home, the Hills were amazed to discover that it was five o'clock in the morning. Somewhere they had lost two hours. Their bodies felt clammy and sore. The trunk of their car had strange circular scratches, which proved to be somewhat radioactive.

Not wanting to be made to feel like fools, the Hills turned in a quiet report to the police and asked that there be no publicity of their sighting.

Name _____

The Lost Hours Activity Sheet

1. Draw a picture of Barney watching the spaceship and the figures inside through his binoculars.

2. Before reading the text on page 104, write down what you think happened to the Hills during those lost hours.

3. Write a creative story about an alien encounter.

4. Do you or do you not think that the Hills should have tried to drive all the way home late at night? Give reasons for your answer.

Name _____

A Personal Encounter

Returning home was not the end of the Hills' story. They knew there was something missing—the two hours they could not account for and the thirty-five miles of the road they could not remember. When Barney's ulcer began to act up and Betty began to have strange nightmares, a friend suggested they see a psychiatrist.

Barney and Betty Hill began treatments under hypnosis, and the story of their amazing encounter began to unfold. Somehow as Barney drove away, he was directed to turn down a side road which was blocked by six beings. The Hills cannot describe these beings very well except that they "talked with their eyes." The beings told the Hills that they would not be harmed and would soon be released if they were cooperative. Both Barney and Betty are a little vague about what happened next, but they do know that they were escorted or carried up a ramp into the spaceship and into separate rooms. There, a doctor who spoke English, examined them thoroughly. Both Barney and Betty had a feeling they were either anesthetized or hypnotized, because the experience had a "fuzzy" quality to it. The next thing the Hills knew, they were back in their car continuing down the highway.

As the story was checked and rechecked by the psychiatrist, he found that the Hills did not change their accounts other than by adding more details. Their drawings of the spaceship and their descriptions of the experience remained almost identical. Both Barney and Betty told the same story of the encounter under hypnosis. Most experts agree that they could have done so only if they had really experienced the same thing!

Name _____

A Personal Encounter Activity Sheet

1. Do some research to find out about hypnosis. Interview a hypnotist to learn if two people could fabricate a story and then tell it repeatedly under hypnosis.

2. Depict the sequence of events in this story in frames of a cartoon strip.

3. Write a more detailed account of the Hills' visit to the spaceship. Include dialogue and detailed descriptions to make it more complete.

4. Write a story entitled "My Own Encounter with a Spaceship."

5. Tell why you do or do not believe the story told by Barney and Betty Hill.

Name _____

UFO Attack?

Early on the morning of August 17, 1979, near the town of Warren, Minnesota, Deputy Val Johnson was patrolling local deserted roads in his police cruiser. Suddenly, Johnson saw a bright light that, strangely enough, did not light up the surrounding trees and ground. The light was very close and was moving slowly.

Thinking it might be smugglers, Johnson maneuvered closer. Without warning, the light leaped directly at him. His car engine stalled, and he slumped over the wheel unconsious.

When Deputy Johnson regained consciousness, he immediately radioed for help. The dispatcher tape recorded his message, a code request for assistance. Johnson had been unconscious for more than forty minutes.

As a result of this encounter, Deputy Johnson had injured eyes, a damaged car, and a wristwatch and dashboard clock that were fourteen minutes slow. A further investigation revealed that the car had been damaged by an external mechanical force, not by heat.

Some people say Deputy Johnson's encounter was a hoax. Some believe that Deputy Johnson was the victim of a prank. Others are certain that his was a valid UFO encounter.

Activities

▲ 1. Illustrate Deputy Johnson's encounter as it might have appeared to an onlooker.

✳ 2. In what ways is Johnson's encounter similar to the Exeter incident? In what ways is it different?

◉ 3. Do you think that the Johnson encounter was genuine, or was it a prank? State your reasons and explain your answer.

Name _____

Project VISIT

On December 20, 1980, Betty Cash saw a huge, bright, diamond-shaped object with flames shooting from beneath it. The object hovered directly over Mrs. Cash's car; and as a result, she was burned and suffered other injuries.

Project VISIT (Vehicle Internal Systems Investigative Team), a group a twelve scientists who try to learn more about UFOs by studying medical evidence, made a complete investigation of the Cash case. They discovered that, on the day following the encounter, Mrs. Cash developed large, knotlike boils on her neck, head, and face. Then she began to lose her hair. Four days later, she began to experience vomiting, diarrhea, swollen eyes, cramps, and loss of energy—all symptoms of radiation exposure. She was treated in a hospital, but it was almost a month before she began to recover.

A Canadian prospector had a similar experience. He encountered a disc-shaped metallic object and subsequently suffered from burns, nausea, vomiting, and swelling.

Some of the places where UFOs have landed have later been found to be burned, to have indentations made by an object of great weight, and to have soil that can no longer absorb water.

In 1971, in Kansas, a sixteen-year-old boy observed a brightly lighted object hovering above the ground. When it departed, he and his parents found a glowing, ring-shaped area on the ground and burns on the tree limbs nearby.

Activities

1. Do research to learn the symptoms of radiation exposure. Then compare Mrs. Cash's symptoms with them to see if they match. What other explanations might be offered for these symptoms?

2. If you were going to develop your own UFO research team, what could you name it so that the name would have an interesting abbreviated form? What would be your basic attitude toward or philosophy about unidentified flying objects and unexplained encounters?

Name _____

Gallup Poll

Sometimes members of a group or organization take a poll, or survey, to find out how people feel about something. Instead of asking everyone, they survey only a small part of the whole group. This small part is called a sample. When poll-taking organizations choose a sample, they want it to be representative of the larger group, so they make certain it contains the same percentage of males and femaies and that it contains people who work in the same jobs, have the same levels of education, and are the same ages as members of the larger group.

One national organization that makes surveys and publishes the results is the Gallup Poll. The Gallup Poll made a report on UFOs in 1966. The poll showed that more than five million Americans believed they had seen a "flying saucer." It also reported that almost half of all Americans believed those UFOs were real, not imaginary. One-third of the people polled believed in life in other worlds, and more women than men believed in UFOs.

A more recent Gallup Poll shows that even more people believe in UFOs today than did in 1966. Fifteen million people now say that they have personally seen a UFO, and 53 percent of the American people say that they believe UFOs exist.

Activities

1. Take your own poll. Write three to five questions about UFOs, select a representative sample of people, ask them what they think, and record the results. Analyze the results and present your findings on a table or chart.

2. Before an election, select a sample and take a poll. On the basis of your results, predict the outcome of the election. After the election, check your predictions against what really happened. How accurate were your predictions? If there is a wide discrepancy, how would you account for it? How representative was your sample?

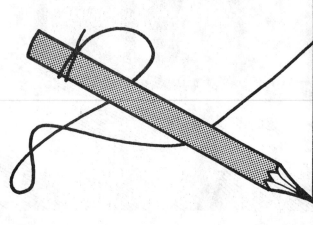

UFO POLL	PERSON SAYS UFOs	DO EXIST	MIGHT EXIST	DO NOT EXIST
1. JANET FRANKLIN			X	
2. ROBERT RICHARDS		X		
3. ERICA BROWN			X	
4. ELIZABETH HANSEN				X
5. STUART ANDREWS				X
6. JASON CAMPBELL		X		
7. RICK JACOBS			X	
8. MARIA FLORES			X	
9. ANDY DAVIS			X	
10. JIM WILLIAMS		X		

Learning More

One way to learn more about UFOs is to find and read any of the following books:

Fuller, John G. *Incident at Exeter.* New York: G. P. Putnam's Sons, 1966.

Keyhoe, Donald. *The Flying Saucers Are Real.* New York: Fawcett, 1950.

Ruppelt, Edward J. *The Report on Unidentified Flying Objects.* Garden City, N.Y.: Doubleday, 1956.

Soule, Garner. *UFOs and IFOs.* New York: G. P. Putnam's Sons, 1967.

White, Dale. *Is Something up There?* Garden City, N.Y.: Doubleday, 1968.

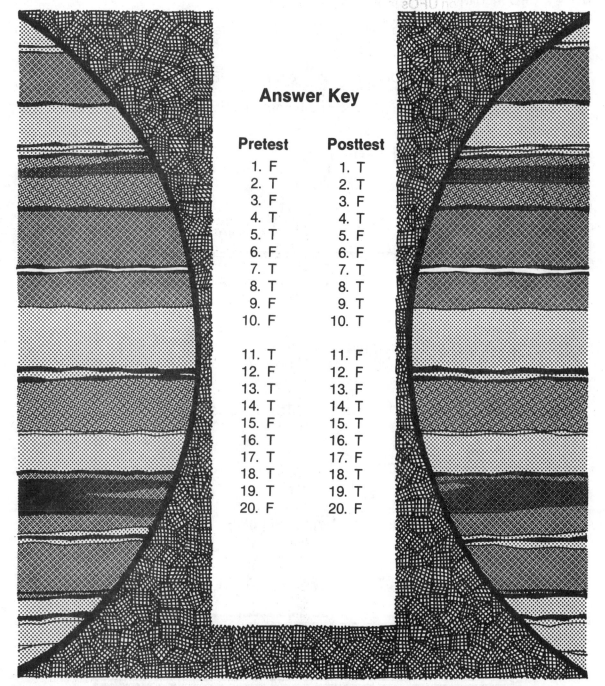

Answer Key

Pretest	Posttest
1. F	1. T
2. T	2. T
3. F	3. F
4. T	4. T
5. T	5. F
6. F	6. F
7. T	7. T
8. T	8. T
9. F	9. T
10. F	10. T
11. T	11. F
12. F	12. F
13. T	13. F
14. T	14. T
15. F	15. T
16. T	16. T
17. T	17. F
18. T	18. T
19. T	19. T
20. F	20. F

Name _____

Correlated Activities

1. Check with your local newspaper to see if there have been any UFO sightings in your area. If so, look up and read the articles about one or more of them.

2. Using a camera, take a fake photograph of a UFO. Then explain to your class how you did it.

3. Using the *Reader's Guide to Periodical Literature* or some other similar resource in your library, locate and read some recent reports of UFO sightings.

4. Make a UFO mobile.

5. Decide whether you do or do not believe in UFOs. Then write an editorial in which you attempt to convince others to share your belief.

6. Write a limerick or other type of humorous poem about UFOs.

7. With a committee, design the first issue of a magazine about UFOs and other related phenomena.

8. Make a time line of well-known UFO sightings.

9. Develop a survey questionnaire about UFOs.

UFOs ARE FOR THE BIRDS

A UFO sighted by Larry

Had citizens frightened and wary.

The scientists came,

And much to their shame,

Discovered it was a canary.

Name _____

Posttest

The following questions are either true or false. If a question is **true**, write a **T** on the line in front of it. If a question is **false**, write an **F** on the line in front of it.

_____ 1. Barney and Betty Hill could not recall much of their experience until they were hypnotized.

_____ 2. Jimmy Carter saw a UFO.

_____ 3. Most astronomers deny the existence of UFOs.

_____ 4. Venus is often mistakenly identified as a UFO.

_____ 5. UFOs were never seen before the invention of the airplane.

_____ 6. A survey sample need not be representative.

_____ 7. Flying saucers are usually described as being disk- or cigar-shaped.

_____ 8. Scientists have proved that, under certain circumstances, ball lightning can exist.

_____ 9. More than fifteen million Americans say they have *seen* a UFO.

_____ 10. IFOs are identified flying objects.

_____ 11. Most UFO reports are hoaxes.

_____ 12. NICAP and Project Blue Book no longer study UFOs.

_____ 13. According to the results of scientific investigation, the Bermuda Triangle is the home of all earth-based UFOs.

_____ 14. Most UFOs eventually become IFOs.

_____ 15. The U.S. government may have had telepathic contact with UFOs.

_____ 16. Captain Mantell chased a balloon to his death.

_____ 17. Meteors are no longer considered to be valid explanations of UFOs.

_____ 18. Pilots have seen small blips merge with big blips on radar.

_____ 19. The air force and airline companies advise their pilots *not* to report UFO sightings to reporters or to the public.

_____ 20. It has been proved that UFOs do not come from outer space.

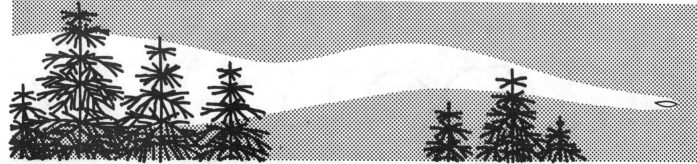

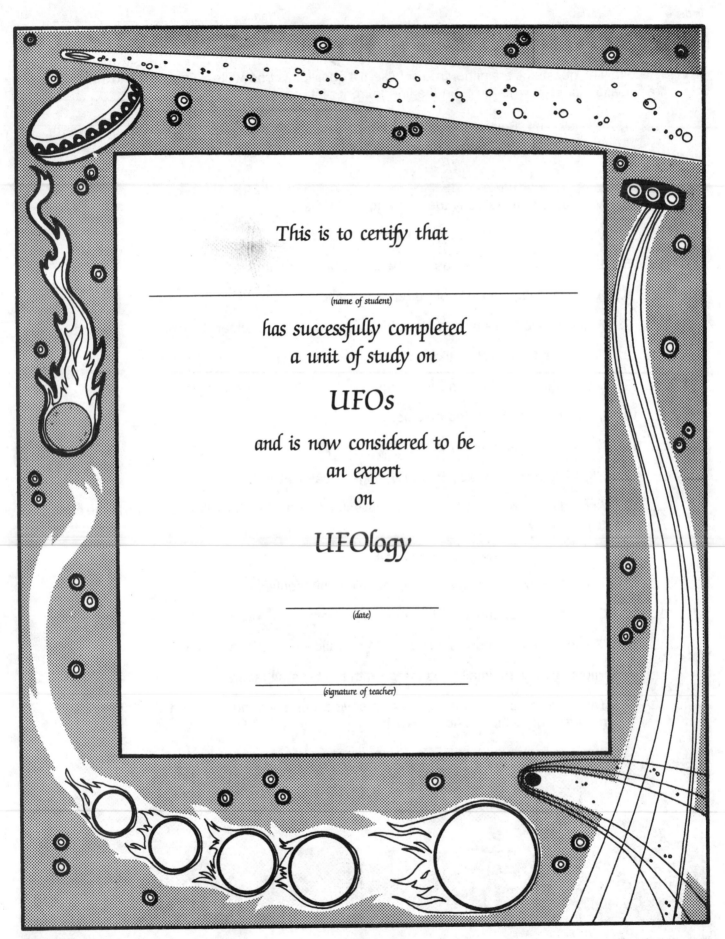

This is to certify that

_____

has successfully completed
a unit of study on

UFOs

and is now considered to be
an expert
on

UFOlogy

_____

_____